PENDULUMS

TASK CARD SERIES

Conceived and
written by
Ron Marson
Illustrated by
Peg Marson

 LEARNING
SYSTEMS

10970 S. Mulino Rd.
Canby OR 97013

NOW YOU CAN PHOTOCOPY!

OLD TASK CARD FORMAT

NEW TASK CARD FORMAT

Dear Educator,

Please excuse our transition . . .

TOPS open-ended task card modules are taking on a new look. Task cards that used to come printed 4-up on heavy index card stock, packaged 2 sets to a zip-lock bag, are now printed 2-up at the back of this single book.

Even though our new cards are printed on lighter book stock, even though we haven't included an extra copy, we can now offer you something much better: You have our permission to make as many photocopies of these task cards as you like, as long as you restrict their use to the students you personally teach. This means you now can (1) incorporate task cards into full-sized worksheets, copying the card at the top of the paper and reserving the bottom for student responses. (2) You can copy and collate task card reference booklets, as many as you need for student use. Or (3) you can make laminated copies to display in your classroom, as before.

It will take some time to fully complete this transition. In the interim we will be shipping TOPS modules as a mixture of both old and new formats. Effective immediately (September 1989) this newer, more liberal photocopy permission applies to all task cards, including our older, heavier, 4-up standards!

Happy sciencing,

Ron Marson
author/publisher

ISBN 0-941008-71-1

Printed on Recycled Paper

CONTENTS

PART I — INTRODUCTION

PART II — TEACHING NOTES

PART III — REPRODUCIBLE STUDENT TASK CARDS

A TOPS Model for Effective Science Teaching...

If science were only a set of explanations and a collection of facts, you could teach it with blackboard and chalk. You could assign students to read chapters and answer the questions that followed. Good students would take notes, read the text, turn in assignments, then give you all this information back again on a final exam. Science is traditionally taught in this manner. Everybody learns the same body of information at the same time. Class togetherness is preserved.

But science is more than this.

Science is also process — a dynamic interaction of rational inquiry and creative play. Scientists probe, poke, handle, observe, question, think up theories, test ideas, jump to conclusions, make mistakes, revise, synthesize, communicate, disagree and discover. Students can understand science as process only if they are free to think and act like scientists, in a classroom that recognizes and honors individual differences.

Science is *both* a traditional body of knowledge *and* an individualized process of creative inquiry. Science as process cannot ignore tradition. We stand on the shoulders of those who have gone before. If each generation reinvents the wheel, there is no time to discover the stars. Nor can traditional science continue to evolve and redefine itself without process. Science without this cutting edge of discovery is a static, dead thing.

Here is a teaching model that combines the best of both elements into one integrated whole. It is only a model. Like any scientific theory, it must give way over time to new and better ideas. We challenge you to incorporate this TOPS model into your own teaching practice. Change it and make it better so it works for you.

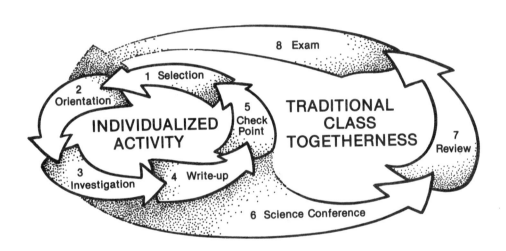

1. SELECTION

Doing TOPS is as easy as selecting the first task card and doing what it says, then the second, then the third, and so on. Working at their own pace, students fall into a natural routine that creates stability and order. They still have questions and problems, to be sure, but students know where they are and where they need to go.

Students generally select task cards in sequence because new concepts build on old ones in a specific order. There are, however, exceptions to this rule: students might *skip* a task that is not challenging; *repeat* a task with doubtful results; *add* a task of their own design to answer original "what would happen if" questions.

2. ORIENTATION

Many students will simply read a task card and immediately understand what to do. Others will require further verbal interpretation. Identify poor readers in your class. When they ask, "What does this mean?" they may be asking in reality, "Will you please read this card aloud?"

With such a diverse range of talent among students, how can you individualize activity and still hope to finish this module as a cohesive group? It's easy. By the time your most advanced students have completed all the task cards, including the enrichment series at the end, your slower students have at least completed the basic core curriculum. This core provides the common

---

background so necessary for meaningful discussion, review and testing on a class basis.

3. INVESTIGATION

Students work through the task cards independently and cooperatively. They follow their own experimental strategies and help each other. You encourage this behavior by helping students only *after* they have tried to help themselves. As a resource person, you work to stay *out* of the center of attention, answering student questions rather than posing teacher questions.

When you need to speak to everyone at once, it is appropriate to interrupt individual task card activity and address the whole class, rather than repeat yourself over and over again. If you plan ahead, you'll find that most interruptions can fit into brief introductory remarks at the beginning of each new period.

4. WRITE-UP

Task cards ask students to explain the "how and why" of things. Write-ups are brief and to the point. Students may accelerate their pace through the task cards by writing these reports out of class.

Students may work alone or in cooperative lab groups. But each one must prepare an original write-up. These must be brought to the teacher for approval as soon as they are completed. Avoid dealing with too many write-ups near the end of the module, by enforcing this simple rule: each write-up must be approved *before* continuing on to the next task card.

5. CHECK POINT

The student and teacher evaluate each write-up together on a pass/no-pass basis. (Thus no time is wasted haggling over grades.) If the student has made reasonable effort consistent with individual ability, the write-up is checked off on a progress chart and included in the student's personal assignment folder or notebook kept on file in class.

Because the student is present when you evaluate, feedback is immediate and effective. A few seconds of this direct student-teacher interaction is surely more effective than 5 minutes worth of margin notes that students may or may not heed. Remember, you don't have to point out every error. Zero in on particulars. If reasonable effort has not been made, direct students to make specific improvements, and see you again for a follow-up check point.

A responsible lab assistant can double the amount of individual attention each student receives. If he or she is mature and respected by your students, have the assistant check the even-numbered write-ups while you check the odd ones. This will balance the work load and insure that all students receive equal treatment.

6. SCIENCE CONFERENCE

After individualized task card activity has ended, this is a time for students to come together, to discuss experimental results, to debate and draw conclusions. Slower students learn about the enrichment activities of faster students. Those who did original investigations, or made unusual discoveries, share this information with their peers, just like scientists at a real conference. This conference is open to films, newspaper articles and community speakers. It is a perfect time to consider the technological and social implications of the topic you are studying.

7. READ AND REVIEW

Does your school have an adopted science textbook? Do parts of your science syllabus still need to be covered? Now is the time to integrate other traditional science resources into your overall program. Your students already share a common background of hands-on lab work. With this shared base of experience, they can now read the text with greater understanding, think and problem-solve more successfully, communicate more effectively.

You might spend just a day on this step or an entire week. Finish with a review of key concepts in preparation for the final exam. Test questions in this module provide an excellent basis for discussion and study.

8. EXAM

Use any combination of the review/test questions, plus questions of your own, to determine how well students have mastered the concepts they've been learning. Those who finish your exam early might begin work on the first activity in the next new TOPS module.

Now that your class has completed a major TOPS learning cycle, it's time to start fresh with a brand new topic. Those who messed up and got behind don't need to stay there. Everyone begins the new topic on an equal footing. This frequent change of pace encourages your students to work hard, to enjoy what they learn, and thereby grow in scientific literacy.

GETTING READY

Here is a checklist of things to think about and preparations to make before your first lesson.

☐ Decide if this TOPS module is the best one to teach next.

TOPS modules are flexible. They can generally be scheduled in any order to meet your own class needs. Some lessons within certain modules, however, do require basic math skills or a knowledge of fundamental laboratory techniques. Review the task cards in this module now if you are not yet familiar with them. Decide whether you should teach any of these other TOPS modules first: *Measuring Length, Graphing, Metric Measure, Weighing* or *Electricity* (before *Magnetism*). It may be that your students already possess these requisite skills or that you can compensate with extra class discussion or special assistance.

☐ Number your task card masters in pencil.

The small number printed in the lower right corner of each task card shows its position within the overall series. If this ordering fits your schedule, copy each number into the blank parentheses directly above it at the top of the card. Be sure to use pencil rather than ink. You may decide to revise, upgrade or rearrange these task cards next time you teach this module. To do this, write your own better ideas on blank 4 x 6 index cards, and renumber them into the task card sequence wherever they fit best. In this manner, your curriculum will adapt and grow as you do.

☐ Copy your task card masters.

You have our permission to reproduce these task cards, for as long as you teach, with only 1 restriction: please limit the distribution of copies you make to the students you personally teach. Encourage other teachers who want to use this module to purchase their *own* copy. This supports TOPS financially, enabling us to continue publishing new TOPS modules for you. For a full list of task card options, please turn to the first task card masters numbered "cards 1-2."

☐ Collect needed materials.

Please see the opposite page.

☐ Organize a way to track completed assignment.

Keep write-ups on file in class. If you lack a vertical file, a box with a brick will serve. File folders or notebooks both make suitable assignment organizers. Students will feel a sense of accomplishment as they see their file folders grow heavy, or their notebooks fill up, with completed assignments. Easy reference and convenient review are assured, since all papers remain in one place.

Ask students to staple a sheet of numbered graph paper to the inside front cover of their file folder or notebook. Use this paper to track each student's progress through the module. Simply initial the corresponding task card number as students turn in each assignment.

☐ Review safety procedures.

Most TOPS experiments are safe even for small children. Certain lessons, however, require heat from a candle flame or Bunsen burner. Others require students to handle sharp objects like scissors, straight pins and razor blades. These task cards should not be attempted by immature students unless they are closely supervised. You might choose instead to turn these experiments into teacher demonstrations.

Unusual hazards are noted in the teaching notes and task cards where appropriate. But the curriculum cannot anticipate irresponsible behavior or negligence. It is ultimately the teacher's responsibility to see that common sense safety rules are followed at all times. Begin with these basic safety rules:

1. Eye Protection: Wear safety goggles when heating liquids or solids to high temperatures.
2. Poisons: Never taste anything unless told to do so.
3. Fire: Keep loose hair or clothing away from flames. Point test tubes which are heating away from your face and your neighbor's.
4. Glass Tubing: Don't force through stoppers. (The teacher should fit glass tubes to stoppers in advance, using a lubricant.)
5. Gas: Light the match first, before turning on the gas.

☐ Communicate your grading expectations.

Whatever your philosophy of grading, your students need to understand the standards you expect and how they will be assessed. Here is a grading scheme that counts individual effort, attitude and overall achievement. We think these 3 components deserve equal weight:

1. Pace (effort): Tally the number of check points you have initialed on the graph paper attached to each student's file folder or science notebook. Low ability students should be able to keep pace with gifted students, since write-ups are evaluated relative to individual performance standards. Students with absences or those who tend to work at a slow pace may (or may not) choose to overcome this disadvantage by assigning themselves more homework out of class.

2. Participation (attitude): This is a subjective grade assigned to reflect each student's attitude and class behavior. Active participators who work to capacity receive high marks. Inactive onlookers, who waste time in class and copy the results of others, receive low marks.

3. Exam (achievement): Task cards point toward generalizations that provide a base for hypothesizing and predicting. A final test over the entire module determines whether students understand relevant theory and can apply it in a predictive way.

Gathering Materials

Listed below is everything you'll need to teach this module. You already have many of these items. The rest are available from your supermarket, drugstore and hardware store. Laboratory supplies may be ordered through a science supply catalog. Hobby stores also carry basic science equipment.

Keep this classification key in mind as you review what's needed:

special in-a-box materials:	general on-the-shelf materials:
Italic type suggests that these materials are unusual. Keep these specialty items in a separate box. After you finish teaching this module, label the box for storage and put it away, ready to use again the next time you teach this module.	Normal type suggests that these materials are common. Keep these basics on shelves or in drawers that are readily accessible to your students. The next TOPS module you teach will likely utilize many of these same materials.
(substituted materials):	*optional materials:
Parentheses enclosing any item suggests a ready substitute. These alternatives may work just as well as the original, perhaps better. Don't be afraid to improvise, to make do with what you have.	An asterisk sets these items apart. They are nice to have, but you can easily live without them. They are probably not worth the extra trip, unless you are gathering other materials as well.

Everything is listed in order of first use. Start gathering at the top of this list and work down. Ask students to bring recycled items from home. The teaching notes may occasionally suggest additional student activity under the heading "Extensions." Materials for these optional experiments are listed neither here nor in the teaching notes. Read the extension itself to find out what new materials, if any, are required.

Needed quantities depend on how many students you have, how you organize them into activity groups, and how you teach. Decide which of these 3 estimates best applies to you, then adjust quantities up or down as necessary:

Q_1 / Q_2 / Q_3

Single Student: Enough for 1 student to do all the experiments.
Individualized Approach: Enough for 30 students informally working in 10 lab groups, all self-paced.
Traditional Approach: Enough for 30 students, organized into 10 lab groups, all doing the same lesson.

KEY:	*special in-a-box materials*	general on-the-shelf materials
	(substituted materials)	*optional materials

Q_1 / Q_2 / Q_3

1/10/10	*cereal boxes — see notes 1*
2/20/20	cups gravel (sand or soil)
1/5/5	rolls masking tape
1/10/10	scissors
1/2/2	spools thread
2/20/20	washers sized to fit quarter inch bolts — see note 1
1/2/3	boxes paper clips of uniform size — see note 1
1/1/1	wall clock with second hand (wrist watches)
1/10/10	stopwatches — see notes 1
1/10/10	hand calculators
1/1/1	*roll thin, bare iron wire, about 30 or 32 gauge*
1/5/10	meter sticks
1/2/5	*wire cutters
1/4/10	batteries, size-D, dead or alive
1/4/10	clothespins
1/10/10	index cards (any straightedge)
1/20/20	straws
4/30/40	straight pins
1/10/10	*plastic lids —see notes 20*
1/2/5	paper punches
1/1/1	working video screen

Sequencing Task Cards

This logic tree shows how all the task cards in this module tie together. In general, students begin at the trunk of the tree and work up through the related branches. As the diagram suggests, the way to upper level activities leads up from lower level activities.

At the teacher's discretion, certain activities can be omitted or sequences changed to meet specific class needs. The only activities that must be completed in sequence are indicated by leaves that open *vertically* into the ones above them. In these cases the lower activity is a prerequisite to the upper.

When possible, students should complete the task cards in the same sequence as numbered. If time is short, however, or certain students need to catch up, you can use the logic tree to identify concept-related *horizontal* activities. Some of these might be omitted since they serve only to reinforce learned concepts rather than introduce new ones.

On the other hand, if students complete all the activities at a certain horizontal concept level, then experience difficulty at the next higher level, you might go back down the logic tree to have students repeat specific key activities for greater reinforcement.

For whatever reason, when you wish to make sequence changes, you'll find this logic tree a valuable reference. Parentheses in the upper right corner of each task card allow you total flexibility. They are left blank so you can pencil in sequence numbers of your own choosing.

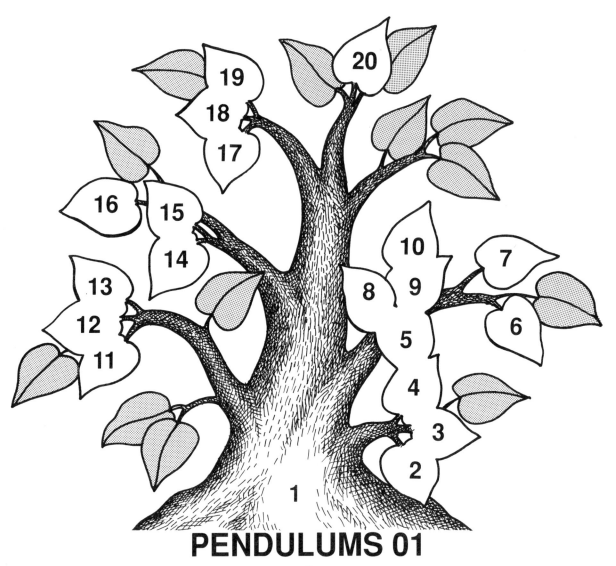

PENDULUMS 01

LONG-RANGE
OBJECTIVES

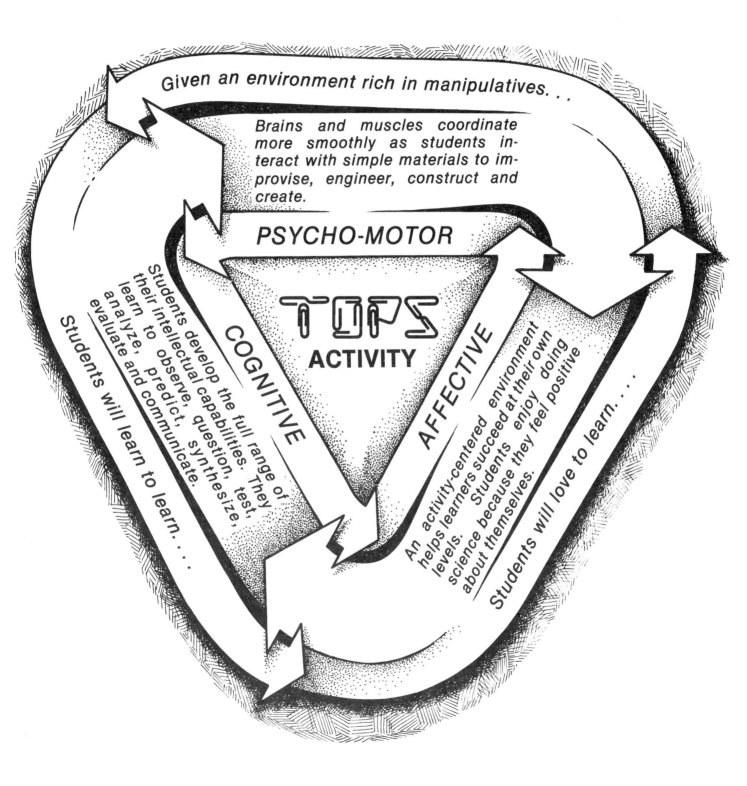

Given an environment rich in manipulatives. . .

Brains and muscles coordinate more smoothly as students interact with simple materials to improvise, engineer, construct and create.

PSYCHO-MOTOR

TOPS
ACTIVITY

COGNITIVE

Students develop the full range of their intellectual capabilities. They learn to observe, question, test, analyze, predict, synthesize, evaluate and communicate.

Students will learn to learn. . . .

AFFECTIVE

An activity-centered environment helps learners succeed at their own levels. Students enjoy doing science because they feel positive about themselves.

Students will love to learn. . . .

Review / Test Questions

Photocopy the questions below. On a separate sheet of blank paper, cut and paste those boxes you want to use as test questions. Include questions of your own design, as well. Crowd all these questions onto a single page for students to answer on another paper, or leave space for student responses after each question, as you wish. Duplicate a class set and your custom-made test is ready to use. Use leftover questions as a review in preparation for the final exam.

task 1-2
A pendulum makes 16 *single* swings in 20 seconds. What is its frequency in cycles per minute?

task 1-3, 8
Using a foot ruler and wristwatch, you collect the following pendulum data:

LENGTH (inches)	1	2	4	6	8	12
FREQUENCY (c/m)	164	132	91	77	67	53

a. Plot these data points on graph paper, then make a graph line.
b. According to your graph, what's the frequency of a 10 inch pendulum?
c. Extrapolate to find the frequency of a 16 inch pendulum.

task 3, 5
A pendulum has a frequency of 120 cycles/minute.
a. What is its frequency in Hz units?
b. What is its period?

task 3-5, 8
Using a meter stick and stop watch, you collect this pendulum data for length *vs* period:

LENGTH (m)	0	1	2	4	8	12
PERIOD (s/c)	0	2.00	2.84	4.02	5.68	6.96

a. Plot these data points on graph paper, then form a graph line.
b. According to your graph, what is the length of a pendulum with a period of 5.00 s/c?
c. Extrapolate to find the length of a pendulum with a period of 8 s/c.

task 4-5
A pendulum swings 20 cycles in 5 seconds.
a. What is its period?
b. What is its frequency in Hz units?

task 4, 6
Summarize how the variables of length, amplitude and bob weight affect the period of a pendulum.

task 6-7
a. Name a variable that affects a thread-and-washer pendulum the same as a spring pendulum.
b. Name another variable that affects them differently.

task 9-12 A
This pendulum data will *not* graph as a straight line.

L = LENGTH (cm)	0	2	6	12
T = PERIOD (s/c)	0	.3	.5	.7

a. Change it *mathematically* so it does.
b. Graph it.
c. Derive a pendulum equation from your graph.

task 9-12 B
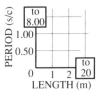
Using a stopwatch, you time the period of a swinging chain for different numbers of beads:

L = LENGTH (beads)	0	10	20	40
T = PERIOD (s/c)	0	.48	.69	.97

a. Develop a data table for L and T^2.
b. Graph your results.
c. Write an equation relating T^2 to L.
d. Use this equation to predict the period of a 100 bead chain.

task 13
Recall that:
$$\sqrt{\frac{L_1}{L_2}} = \frac{T_1}{T_2}$$
Use the data in this table to find √6.

LENGTH (cm)	0	2	6	12
PERIOD (s/c)	0	.29	.51	.71

task 14-15 A
Your car is stuck in a deep rut. To free it should you push straight forward, or rock it back and forth? Explain.

task 14-15 B
A short pendulum has exactly twice the frequency of a long pendulum. Suppose you connect these with a straw energy bridge, then start the long one swinging. What happens to the short straw? Explain.

task 16
A 12 cm pendulum is taped 4 cm from the bottom of a cupboard and then set in motion so it swings underneath. Use this data table for other pendulums to calculate its particular frequency.
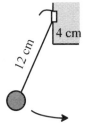

LENGTH (cm)	0	4	8	12
PERIOD (s/c)	0	.42	.58	.70

task 16-17
A 90 cm pendulum is attached to a 60 cm cupboard. The bob is pulled out as shown, then released. Will it strike the bottom of the cupboard? If so, where? Explain.

task 17-19 A
A pendulum is gently pushed to maintain its maximum amplitude at an energetic 90°. Its KE (kinetic energy) changes with amplitude like this:
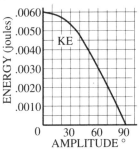
a. Why does KE reach a maximum at 0° and a minimum at 90°?
b. Draw another curve on this same graph to represent the pendulum's PE (potential energy).
c. At what amplitude does KE = PE?

task 17-19 B
A weight tied to a thread loop is gently twirled around a straw like this:
a. Where does this system have maximum potential energy? Maximum kinetic energy? Explain.
b. Where does this system have minimum potential energy? Minimum kinetic energy? Explain.
c. Compare and contrast this system to a normal back-and-forth pendulum.

task 20
A wheel is turned faster and faster in front of a video screen until its 24 spokes appear to stand still. A tag on its rim is found to make 10 turns in 4 seconds. Calculate the refresh frequency of this video screen.

Answers

task 1-2

$$\text{freq.} = \frac{16 \text{ swings}}{20 \text{ seconds}} = \frac{8 \text{ c}}{20 \text{ s}} = 24 \text{ c/m}$$

task 1-3, 8

a.
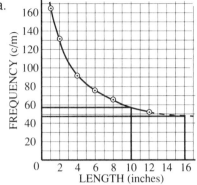

b. 10 inch: 57 c/m

c. 16 inch extrapolation: 48 c/m

task 3, 5

a. $\dfrac{120 \text{ c}}{1 \text{ m}} \times \dfrac{1 \text{ m}}{60 \text{ s}} = \dfrac{2 \text{ c}}{1 \text{ s}} = 2 \text{ Hz}$

b. $\text{period} = \dfrac{1}{\text{freq.}} = \dfrac{1 \text{ s}}{2 \text{ c}} = .5 \text{ s/c}$

task 3-5, 8

a.
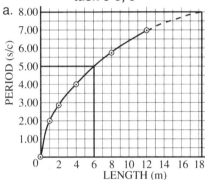

b. 5.00 s/c: 6.0 meters

c. 8 s/c extrapolation: 18.3 meters

task 4-5

a. $\text{period} = \dfrac{5 \text{ s}}{20 \text{ c}} = .25 \text{ s/c}$

b. $\text{freq.} = \dfrac{1}{\text{per.}} = \dfrac{20 \text{ c}}{5 \text{ s}} = 4 \text{ s/c} = 4 \text{ Hz}$

task 4, 6

The period of a pendulum increases with increasing length; decreases with decreasing length. Changes in amplitude produce a similar but much smaller effect. Changes in bob weight have no effect on the period at all.

task 6-7

a. The periods of both pendulums increase with increasing length.

b. Increasing bob weight increases the period of a spring pendulum, but leaves the period of a thread-and-washer pendulum unchanged.

task 9-12 A

a.
L = LENGTH (cm)	0	2	6	12
T^2 = PERIOD^2 (s/c)^2	0	.09	.25	.49

b.
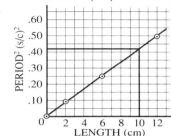

c. The ratio of variables for any point on a straight graph line is constant. Thus for $(L, T^2) = (10, .42)$:
$10 T^2 = .42 L$ or $T^2 = .042 L$ or $L = 24 T^2$.

task 9-12 B

a.
L (beads)	0	10	20	40
T^2 (s/c)^2	0	.23	.48	.94

b.
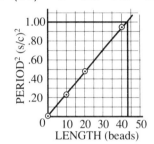

c. The ratio of variables for any point on a straight graph line is constant. Thus for $(L, T^2) = (43, 1.00)$:
$43 T^2 = 1.00 L$ or $T^2 = .023 L$.

d. $T = \sqrt{.023 \, L} = \sqrt{.023 \, (100)} = 1.5 \text{ s/c}$

task 13

$$\sqrt{6} = \sqrt{\frac{12}{2}} = \frac{.71}{.29} = 2.45$$

task 14-15 A

Rock the car in phase with its natural frequency. In this manner you can add energy little by little, until the car stores enough to rock free.

task 14-15 B

Because the short pendulum has twice the frequency, any energy gain it makes when the long pendulum swings in one direction is immediately given up as this long pendulum swings back again. Thus the short pendulum should hardly move at all, while the long pendulum remains swinging.

task 16

This 2-pivot pendulum swings at a length of 12 cm through half its cycle; at a length of 8 cm through its other half. Its overall period is the average:

$$\frac{.58 \text{ s/c} + .70 \text{ s/c}}{2} = .64 \text{ s/c}$$

task 16-17

The bob will strike the bottom of the cupboard, 30 cm from where the thread bends under its outside edge. Potential energy, added to the pendulum bob by virtue of its raised position, boosts it to nearly the same height under the cupboard (less minor losses due to air resistance).

task 17-19 A

a. KE reaches a maximum at 0° because the pendulum bob moves fastest at the bottom of its swing. It reaches a minimum at 90° because it stops at this amplitude, at the top of each swing.

b.
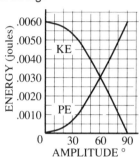

c. KE = PE = 60°.

task 17-19 B

a. The system has maximum PE at the top of its arc, its highest point. It has maximum KE at the bottom of its arc, where it moves most rapidly.

b. The system has minimum PE at the bottom of its arc, its lowest point. It has minimum KE at the top of its arc, where it moves most slowly.

c. PE + KE is constant in both systems (as long as enough energy is added to overcome friction), and PE = 0 at the bottom of their respective cycles. At the top of their cycles, however, the washer stops in the pendulum system (KE = 0) but only slows down in the orbiting system (KE > 0).

task 20

Time for 10 wheel revolutions = 4 s

Period of wheel = .4 s/c

Spoke-to-spoke time = $\dfrac{.4 \text{ s/c}}{24}$

Refresh period = $\dfrac{.4 \text{ s}}{24 \text{ c}}$ = .016 s/c

Refresh frequency = $\dfrac{24 \text{ c}}{.4 \text{ s}}$ = 60 c/s

H

TEACHING NOTES
For Activities 1-20

Task Objective (TO) construct a cereal-box pendulum support with a length and amplitude background grid for use in activities throughout this module.

PENDULUM BOX   ○   Pendulums (   )

1. Fill an empty cereal box about 1/6 full of gravel. Tape it closed, then tip it on its side.

2. Cut out the Pendulum Grid. Fold it back on the dotted line to fit neatly over the upper edge of your box. Tape in place.

3. Fold a tab of tape over the double-loop end of a paper clip. *Lightly* tape it to the center top of the box with its taped "nose" sticking out.

4. Tie thread to a washer. Insert this thread into a slit that you cut in the tape tab to the center "nose" of the clip. Tilt the box forward to let the washer unwind.

5. Tape the thread at the top of the box so its washer centers perfectly over the 12 cm circle (adjust the clip as needed). Now release your pendulum at an *amplitude* of 10°.
   a. Check that the pendulum swings for at least 1 minute without stopping. Adjust, if necessary, for minimum friction with maximum closeness to the box. Then tape the clip (not the pendulum thread) firmly in place.
   b. Write your name on top.

1

Answers / Notes

1. *Don't overfill. This will bulge out the sides of the box, possibly interfering with the swing of the pendulum.*

3. *The overhanging paper clip support is taped lightly for now. It may require fine adjustments in step 5a before being taped more permanently in place.*

5. *Secure this thread with a second piece of tape, overlaying the first layer that already holds the paper clip.*

5a. *The washer should clear the box by a millimeter or so when swinging parallel to its surface. It should show little preference for twisting right or left, only lightly brushing the box's surface when it turns. After the paper clip is adjusted perfectly, secure it with additional tape. If the pendulum thread is inadvertently taped to the box along with the paper clip, simply pull it free. There is no need to retape.*

Materials

☐ A Pendulum Grid. Photocopy this from the supplementary page at the back of this book.
☐ A cereal box. We prefer a 2 pound Post Grape-Nuts box for its sturdy construction, and have sized our pendulum grid to fit it perfectly. Any larger box with square corners and flat sides will also serve.
☐ Gravel, sand or dirt. This provides ballast to prevent box movement as the pendulum swings.
☐ Masking tape.
☐ Scissors.
☐ Thread.
☐ Uniform washers that fit 1/4 inch bolts. The circles on our Pendulum Grid match their 3/8 inch holes. While other sizes may be used in initial activities, they are not suitable for activities 17-19.
☐ A flat working surface.
☐ Paper clips of uniform size. We use No. 1 Gem paper clips about this size. If your particular brand is longer or shorter than this, tell your class that the "nose" of the clip should stick out about 5 mm.
☐ A stopwatch. A clock with a second hand may be conveniently substituted in the first two activities, but not in experiments that follow. Digital stopwatches are relatively inexpensive, well worth the gains in speed and accuracy that your students will realize throughout this module.

(TO) find the frequency of a pendulum in cycles per minute for various lengths. To summarize how the frequency of a pendulum varies with length.

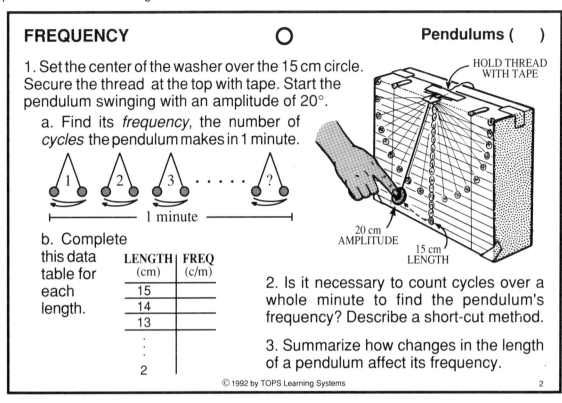

FREQUENCY ○ **Pendulums ( )**

1. Set the center of the washer over the 15 cm circle. Secure the thread at the top with tape. Start the pendulum swinging with an amplitude of 20°.

HOLD THREAD WITH TAPE

a. Find its *frequency*, the number of *cycles* the pendulum makes in 1 minute.

1   2   3   · · · · ·   ?

├─────── 1 minute ───────┤

b. Complete this data table for each length.

20 cm AMPLITUDE

15 cm LENGTH

LENGTH (cm)	FREQ (c/m)
15	
14	
13	
⋮	
2	

2. Is it necessary to count cycles over a whole minute to find the pendulum's frequency? Describe a short-cut method.

3. Summarize how changes in the length of a pendulum affect its frequency.

© 1992 by TOPS Learning Systems   2

Answers / Notes

1a. *The 15 cm pendulum makes 77 cycles per minute. That is, it swings back and forth (returning near its starting position each time), 77 times in 1 minute.*

1b.

LENGTH (cm)	FREQ (c/m)
15	77
14	79
13	82
12	85
11	89
10	93
9	98
8	104
7	110
6	118
5	130
4	144
3	164
2	208

2. No. Count the number of cycles in 30 seconds and multiply by 2; or the number of cycles in 15 seconds and multiply by 4.

Counting cycles over shorter time intervals is a trade-off. While efficiency increases, accuracy is lost. The amplitudes of very short pendulums, however, decay much too rapidly to be counted over a full minute.

3. The length of a pendulum and its frequency vary in *opposite* directions: as length decreases, frequency increases; as length increases, frequency decreases.

Materials

☐ The pendulum box just constructed.
☐ Masking tape.
☐ Scissors.
☐ A stopwatch or clock with a second hand.

(TO) convert pendulum frequencies from cycles per minute to cycles per second, or hertz units. To graph how the frequency of a pendulum varies with length.

LENGTH *vs* FREQUENCY ⚪   Pendulums (   )

1. Frequency is usually measured in units called *hertz* (Hz). If a pendulum vibrates 1 cycle every second, it has a frequency of 1 Hz.

    a. A pendulum has a frequency of 1.5 Hz. How many cycles does it complete in 1 minute?

    b. A pendulum has a frequency of 77 c/m. What is its frequency in hertz units?

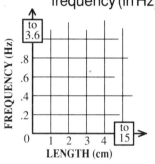

2. Copy your results from the last activity into a new table. Then convert the frequency for each pendulum length from cycles/minute to hertz units.

LENGTH (cm)	FREQ (c/m)	FREQ (Hz=c/s)
15		
14		
13		
⋮		
2		

3. Graph length (in cm) *vs* frequency (in Hz).

© 1992 by TOPS Learning Systems   3

Answers / Notes

1a. $1.5 \text{ Hz} = \dfrac{1.5 \text{ c}}{1 \text{ s}}$

    $\dfrac{1.5 \text{ c}}{1 \text{ s}} \times 60 \text{ s} = 90 \text{ c}$

1b. $\dfrac{77 \text{ c}}{1 \text{ m}} \times \dfrac{1 \text{ m}}{60 \text{ s}} = 1.28 \text{ Hz}$

2.

LENGTH (cm)	FREQ (c/m)	FREQ (Hz=c/s)
15	77	1.28
14	79	1.32
13	82	1.37
12	85	1.42
11	89	1.48
10	93	1.55
9	98	1.63
8	104	1.73
7	110	1.83
6	118	1.97
5	130	2.17
4	144	2.40
3	164	2.73
2	208	3.47

3.

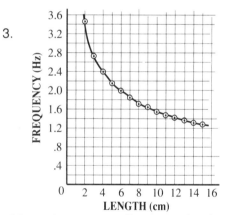

Measuring errors will scatter the data points somewhat. Your students should draw the best possible smooth line among *them, not necessarily through* every *point. This line should never obscure the data point itself. Hence, each one is circled.*

    Points that are especially wide of the mark may have been plotted or measured in error and should be rechecked. Emphasize that each space on the vertical frequency scale is worth .2 Hz, not .1 Hz. It may help your students to more accurately place each data point if they first divide each space they are estimating into two equal halves with a pencil mark. This allows them to mentally subdivide the remaining space by 10 instead of by 20.

Materials

☐ A calculator.
☐ The completed data table from the previous activity.
☐ Graph paper. Photocopy this from the supplementary page at the back of this book. Each student will need about 6 grids to complete all the graphs in this module.

(TO) find the period of a pendulum in seconds per cycle for various lengths. To summarize how the period of a pendulum varies with length.

PERIOD ◯ Pendulums ( )

1. Fix the length of your pendulum at 15 cm.

   a. Use a stopwatch to time the number of seconds required to complete 10 cycles. Practice until you consistently get the same result within a range of .10 second.

   b. Complete the middle column of the data table for each length.

LENGTH (cm)	TIME for 10 cycles (s)	PERIOD (s/c)
15		
14		
13		
⋮		
2		

2. The *period* of a pendulum is the time (in seconds) needed to complete 1 cycle. Enter the period for each length in column 3.

$$Period = \frac{no.\ of\ seconds}{1\ cycle}$$

3. Summarize how changes in the length of a pendulum affects its period. Is this how length affects frequency?

4

Introduction

Demonstrate how to accurately time the pendulum with a stopwatch. First set it in motion, then on the upswing (either to the right or to the left) count…"3, 2, 1, 0, 1, 2, 3, 4, 5, 6, 7, 8, 9 10."

|Start timing . . .   . . . |end timing.

This gives you the time for 10 cycles. Divide by 10 to find the time for 1 second — the period. This method is quick and accurate. It should be used in all stopwatch timings. Without stopwatches, your class will need to count cycles over a longer fixed interval of time, say 30 seconds, then do long division on a calculator.

Answers / Notes

1-2.
LENGTH (cm)	TIME for 10 cycles (s)	PERIOD (s/c)
15	7.83	.783
14	7.57	.757
13	7.30	.730
12	7.02	.702
11	6.76	.676
10	6.37	.637
9	6.09	.609
8	5.74	.574
7	5.38	.538
6	5.08	.508
5	4.68	.468
4	4.23	.423
3	3.69	.369
2	3.13	.313

3. The length of a pendulum and its period vary in the *same* direction: as length increases, so does the period; as length decreases, so does the period. Length and frequency, by contrast, vary in opposite directions.

Materials

☐ The pendulum box.
☐ A stopwatch.

(TO) understand the inverse relationship between period and frequency, both mathematically and graphically.

LENGTH *vs* PERIOD ○   Pendulums ( )

1. Copy your results from the last two activities into a new data table with *increasing* lengths.

2. How are frequencies and periods related? Experiment by dividing each of them into 1. What do you notice?

3. Write an equation that relates frequency to period; period to frequency.

4. Make a graph as shown, with extra length for later use. Plot *length vs period*, then draw a smooth curve.

5. Compare this graph line to its *inverse* in activity 3. What do you see?

6. Remember how you measured the data in columns 2 and 3. Which measurements do you think contain less experimental error? Explain.

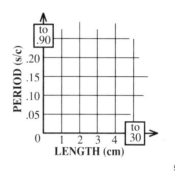

LENGTH (cm)	FREQ. (c/s=Hz)	PERIOD (s/c)
0	—	0
2		
3		
⋮		
15		

© 1992 by TOPS Learning Systems   5

Answers / Notes

1.

LENGTH (cm)	FREQ. (c/s=Hz)	PERIOD (s/c)
0	—	0
2	3.47	.313
3	2.73	.369
4	2.40	.423
5	2.17	.468
6	1.97	.508
7	1.83	.538
8	1.73	.574
9	1.63	.609
10	1.55	.637
11	1.48	.676
12	1.42	.702
13	1.37	.730
14	1.32	.757
15	1.28	.783

2. Each frequency divided into 1 gets reasonably close to its corresponding period; each period divided into 1 approximates its frequency.

3. Frequency = 1/Period;   Period = 1/Frequency.

4.

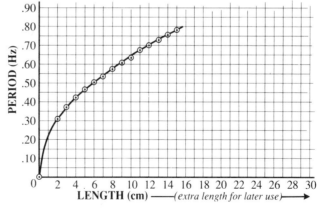

5. Both graphs have the same general shape in a mirror-image orientation: the frequency graph sweeps downward with increasing length in an ever moderating curve, while the period graph sweeps upward in an ever moderating curve.

6. *This step asks students to hypothesize. Accept all thoughtful answers.*
   The frequency data is more accurate, considering that the pendulum cycles were counted over longer time intervals — 15 to 60 seconds as compared with 3 to 8 seconds. The period time intervals, however, end precisely after the 10th cycle. There is no mid-swing rounding off. Overall, we think the frequency data is most accurate for long pendulums; period data for short pendulums.

Materials

☐ Results from activities 3 and 4.
☐ A calculator.
☐ The pendulum box.
☐ A stopwatch.
☐ Graph paper.

(TO) evaluate the relative effects of length, amplitude and bob weight on the period of a pendulum.

AMPLITUDE & BOB WEIGHT ○   Pendulums (   )

1. Set your pendulum at 12 cm.

a. Measure the period of this pendulum when released at each angle of amplitude. Time 10 cycles with a stopwatch as before, then divide by 10 to compute the period.

AMPLI-TUDE (°)	PERIOD (s/c)
10	
30	
50	
70	
90	

b. Do changing *amplitudes* affect a pendulum's period? How does this compare to changing *length*?

2. Reset your pendulum at 16 cm.

ROLLED TAPE

a. Add extra washers to the pendulum bob with small rolls of tape. Time the periods for different bob weights when released at a constant 20° amplitude.

BOB WEIGHT (washers)	PERIOD (s/c)
1	
2	
3	
4	
5	

b. Do changes in *bob weight* affect a pendulum's period? Explain.

MASS OF BOB — LENGTH — AMPLITUDE

3. Summarize how these three *variables* affect the period of a pendulum.

6

Answers / Notes

1a.

AMPLI-TUDE (°)	PERIOD (s/c)
10	.701
30	.708
50	.728
70	.756
90	.764

1b. As the amplitude of the pendulum increases, its period also increases to a small but significant degree. This increase, however, is much less pronounced than increases due to length.

It is more difficult to detect this variation when timing without a stopwatch over a fixed time interval, because there is a natural tendency to round off the counted cycles to the nearest whole number.

2a. *To keep the washer weights evenly distributed, students should add them to both sides of the washer, in alternating fashion.*

BOB WEIGHT (washers)	PERIOD (s/c)
1	.783
2	.792
3	.783
4	.782
5	.788

2b. Changes in bob weight do not cause any measurable changes in the period. The small variations in time that do appear are random, the result of experimental error.

3. The period of a pendulum is greatly influenced by length, increasing and decreasing as its length increases and decreases. Changes in amplitude produce a similar but much smaller effect. Changes in bob weight have no effect on the period at all.

Materials

☐ The pendulum box.
☐ A stopwatch.
☐ Four additional washers.
☐ Masking tape.
☐ Scissors.

(TO) apply concepts and skills in the study of washer pendulums to a new oscillating system — a spring system.

BOINGGG! ○ Pendulums ( )

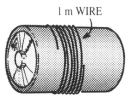
1 m WIRE

1. Wrap 1 meter of thin wire evenly around a size-D battery to make a coil spring.

2. Pull out the arm of a paper clip a little to form a hook. Attach it to one end of your spring.

3. Clamp the other end of your spring to a clothespin that is taped on your cereal box. Set the box at the edge of your table so the spring falls over the edge.

4. Investigate how different variables (bob weight, length, etc.) affect the period of a spring pendulum. Compare your result to washer pendulums. Your write-up should include at least 1 graph.

5. Carefully remove the clothespin from your pendulum box when you finish.

VARIABLES?

7

Answers / Notes

4.

BOB WEIGHT (clips)	PERIOD (s/c)
1	.386
2	.495
3	.580
4	.646
5	.716
6	.759
7	.799
8	.833
9	.846
10	.850

BOB WEIGHT:

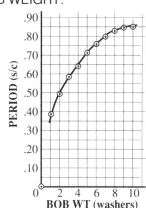

As the bob weight on a spring increases or decreases, so does its period. This variable is not important for washer pendulums.

LENGTH: As the length of the spring increases or decreases, so does its period. This variable affects washer pendulums in a similar way. *(This variation can be graphed by marking off equal lengths with a felt pen or white correction fluid while the wire is still coiled around the battery.)*

AMPLITUDE: The amplitude of the oscillating spring seems to have no measurable effect on its period. Unlike washer pendulums, minor variations seem random.

COIL TIGHTNESS: With heavy paper clip loads, the spring tends to stretch out and lose its bounce. This causes it to oscillate more rapidly, thus decreasing its period. *(Expect most students to overlook this variable. Because it is not easily controlled, graphs of bob weight vs period may vary widely.)*

Materials

☐ Thin, bare iron wire, about 30 or 32 gauge. Test your particular wire in advance to be sure that it forms springs with periods that are slow enough to time; that it responds well to paper clip increments of weight change.
☐ A meter stick.
☐ Wire cutters (optional). You can also break the wire by repeatedly bending it back and forth.
☐ A size-D battery, dead or alive.

☐ Paper clips.
☐ A clothespin and masking tape.
☐ The pendulum box. Any steady object that you can tape a clothespin to will work as long as the spring is raised high enough to remain off the floor with a full load of paper clips.
☐ A stopwatch.
☐ Graph paper.

(TO) extrapolate the graph line of length *vs* period to longer lengths. To evaluate the accuracy of this prediction.

EXTRAPOLATE ○ Pendulums ( )

1. Extrapolate (extend) your graph line in activity 5 with a dashed line: draw your best guess based on how the curve seems to change.

2. Based on your extrapolation, *predict* what pendulum length will tick like a clock — exactly 1 second per cycle.

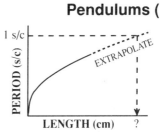

3. Fold a tape handle *loosely* over thread tied to a washer. Slide it to make a "clock" pendulum with your predicted length, as measured from the center of the bob to the edge of the tape (called the *pivot*).

TAPE HANDLE ← *SLIDE ALONG THREAD* →

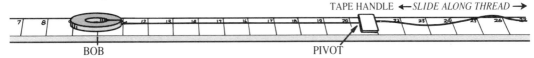

BOB   PIVOT

a. Swing this pendulum clock by its tape pivot. How close does it come to ticking 1 s/c?

b. Slide the pivot up or down until your "clock" keeps good time. Record its length as a hard data point on your graph.

4. Change your pendulum's length to locate 2 more hard data points in the extrapolated area of your graph. Evaluate the accuracy of your extrapolation. (*Don't* redraw your dashed line.)

© 1992 by TOPS Learning Systems   8

Answers / Notes

1-4.

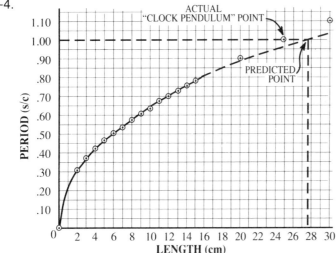

2. Our extrapolation suggests that a "clock" pendulum ticking with a period of 1 second per cycle has a length of 27.7 cm.

3a. A pendulum with our particular length takes 1.071 seconds to complete 1 cycle. It ticks a little too slow.

3b. A "clock" pendulum that accurately measures time has a length of 24.8 cm, give or take .3 cm. Again, this distance should be measured from the center of the washer to the pivot.

4. *Students should find the period of at least two more pendulums within the length range of 15 cm to 30 cm, and plot them on the graph. They should leave their original extrapolation in place, then evaluate its accuracy.*

Extrapolations will vary (ours was too low), since it is difficult to judge just how rapidly the curve moderates or flattens.

Materials

☐ The graph from activity 5.
☐ A washer and thread.
☐ Scissors.
☐ A meter stick.
☐ Masking tape.
☐ A stopwatch.
☐ A clock or wristwatch with a second hand (optional). This is easier to use in step 2b than a digital stopwatch.

(TO) graph how the length of a pendulum varies with the square of its period. To observe that the ratio of these variables yields a constant number.

SQUARE IT ◯ Pendulums (   )

1. Copy the period data from activity 5 into this new table:

2. Find the square of each period: use a calculator to multiply the period by itself, then enter each result (to three figures) in column 3.

3. Graph your data from columns 1 and 3.

   a. Your points will distribute into a fairly straight line, with some scattering due to experimental error. Which points do you trust the most? The least? Explain.

   b. Use a thread to draw the best possible straight line among your data points.

4. Each point on your graph line relates a unique pendulum length (L) to the square of its particular period (T^2).

   a. Compute the ratio $\mathbf{L/T^2}$ for T^2 = .20, .40, and .60.

   b. What always seems true?

Activity 5 last column

LENGTH $L=cm$	PERIOD $T=s/c$	PERIOD^2 $T^2=(s/c)^2$
0		
2		
3		
$\vdots$		
15		

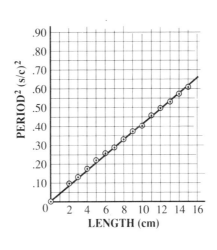

BEST COMPROMISE...

© 1992 by TOPS Learning Systems   9

Answers / Notes

1-3.

LENGTH $L=cm$	PERIOD $T=s/c$	PERIOD^2 $T^2=(s/c)^2$
0	0	0
2	.313	.098
3	.369	.136
4	.423	.179
5	.468	.219
6	.508	.258
7	.538	.289
8	.574	.329
9	.609	.371
10	.637	.406
11	.676	.457
12	.702	.493
13	.730	.533
14	.757	.573
15	.783	.613

Graph: PERIOD^2 (s/c)^2 (y-axis, .10 to .90) vs LENGTH (cm) (x-axis, 2 to 16). Data points form a straight line.

3a. Data points for longer lengths are more reliable than data points for shorter lengths, because the pendulum swings over a longer time interval and at a slower pace that is more easily tracked. *(The point at [0,0], however, is a given with no margin of error at all. A pendulum with no length has an infinitely short period.)*

3b. *Students should position one end of the thread at (0,0) then align the other end so that as many points as possible (especially those of longer lengths) remain near or under the straightened thread.*

4a. $\dfrac{L}{T^2} = \dfrac{4.8}{.20} = 24.0$ $\dfrac{L}{T^2} = \dfrac{9.7}{.40} = 24.3$ $\dfrac{L}{T^2} = \dfrac{14.5}{.60} = 24.2$

4b. The ratio is always close to 24. *(The most ideal result is 25, a constant that will be important in the next activity.)*

This constant does have units: 25 cm/sec^2. While units are an extremely important part of any measurement, we have not included them when substituted into mathematical formulas, for the sake of simplicity.

Materials

☐ The data table from activity 5.
☐ A calculator.
☐ Graph paper.
☐ Thread.
☐ An index card or straightedge.

(TO) derive an equation that relates the length of a pendulum to its period. To apply this equation in a predictive way and confirm that it is valid.

PENDULUM EQUATION　　　○　　　　Pendulums ( )

1. Flag a pendulum with *skinny* strips of masking tape at these lengths. Measure from the center of the bob to the center of each flag.

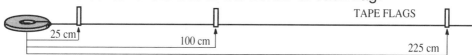

TAPE FLAGS

25 cm　　　　100 cm　　　　225 cm

2. Swing the pendulum from each flag while a friend counts off seconds on a clock.

...2...3...

L (cm)	T (s/c)
0	
25	
100	
225	

EQUATION?

   a. Each pendulum length measures seconds in a different way. Describe each.
   b. Use whole numbers to complete this table. L stands for Length; T stands for Time measured over the length of 1 period.

3. Use some combination of mathematical operations (+, -, x, ÷, n^2, $\sqrt{}$) to get from each T to its corresponding L. (Hint: recall your findings in the previous activity.)

4. Use your equation to calculate L when T = .5 s/c; when T = 4 s/c. Confirm at least one of your results by experiment; both, if possible.

5. Imagine launching off on a 1 km rope swing hanging from a sky hook. How many seconds would you ride before returning to your starting point?

© 1992 by TOPS Learning Systems　　　　　　　　　10

Answers / Notes

2a. 25 cm pendulum: makes 1 cycle every second.
    100 cm pendulum: makes 1 cycle every 2 seconds, or 1 swing every second.
    225 cm pendulum: makes 1 cycle every 3 seconds.

2b.
L (cm)	T (s/c)
0	0
25	1
100	2
225	3

3. Square each T, then multiply by 25:
$$25 (T^2) = L$$

In theory, this multiple is not quite equal to 25. The formula for a simple pendulum swinging at small amplitudes from a line with negligible mass is given by:

$$T^2 = 4\pi^2 L/g$$
$$(g/4\pi^2)(T^2) = L$$
$$(980/4\pi^2)(T^2) = L$$
$$24.8\, T^2 = L$$

4. When T = .5 s/c, L = 25 (.5)² = 6.25 cm.
   When T = 4 s/c, L = 25 (4)² = 400 cm.

A dot on the pendulum box in the lower part of the 6 cm circle indicates a length of 6.25 cm. When the washer is centered over this dot it swings, as predicted, about 2 cycles each second. Similarly, if your students can find a place to safely swing a washer from 4 meters of thread, they will measure a frequency of 4 seconds per cycle.

5. *This calculation assumes an extraordinary light-weight, high-tech rope.*

$$T^2 = L/25, \text{ where } L = 1 \text{ km or } 100,000 \text{ cm}$$
$$T^2 = 4,000$$
$$T = \sqrt{4,000} = 63 \text{ seconds}$$

Materials

☐ Thread and scissors.
☐ A washer.
☐ Masking tape.
☐ A meter stick.

☐ A clock with a second hand. Or substitute a stopwatch.
☐ A stable chair to stand on.
☐ The pendulum box.

☐ Access to a second story window or balcony, a stairwell, or perhaps the bleachers in your school's gym is optional. Otherwise the 4 second period of a 4 meter pendulum must remain theoretical.

(TO) graph how the period of a paper-clip chain changes with length. To compare its graph line with a thread and washer pendulum.

CHAIN LINKS (1) ○ Pendulums (   )

1. Paper clips link to make a chain pendulum. Develop a data table and graph to explore the relationship between length (in paper clips) and period (in s/c).

THIS IS A **6 CLIP** CHAIN:

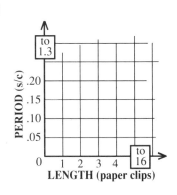

2. How do your results compare with the washer pendulum you studied earlier?

11

Answers / Notes

1.

LENGTH (paper clips)	PERIOD (s/c)
0	0
1	.310
2	.412
3	.510
4	.599
5	.659
6	.730
7	.782
8	.839
9	.884
12	1.031
16	1.192

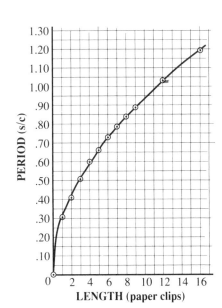

2. The paper-clip chain graphs into the same basic shape as a washer pendulum. Its period increases with increasing length, more rapidly at shorter lengths, less rapidly at longer lengths.

Materials
☐ Paper clips of uniform size.
☐ A stopwatch.
☐ Graph paper.

(TO) apply concepts and skills learned with thread pendulums to paper clip pendulums. To develop an equation relating the period of a paper clip chain to the number of clips it contains.

CHAIN LINKS (2) ○ Pendulums (   )

1. Determine how the length (L) of a paper-clip chain varies directly with the square of its period (T^2). Develop a data table and graph.

2. If L = 10 clips, read T^2 from your graph.
   a. Find the ratio L/T^2 on a calculator.
   b. Recall the equation you developed for a washer pendulum. Write a similar equation for paper-clip pendulums.

3. Use your equation to find the frequency of a 20 clip chain. Verify your answer with a stopwatch.

4. How many paper clips should you link together to make a chain that requires 1 whole minute to complete just 1 cycle?

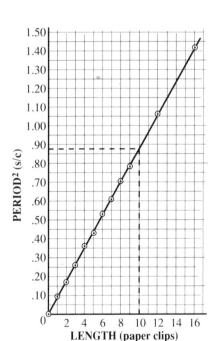

© 1992 by TOPS Learning Systems   12

Answers / Notes

1.   Activity 11

LENGTH (paper clips)	PERIOD (s/c)	PERIOD^2 (s/c)^2
0	0	0
1	.310	.096
2	.412	.170
3	.510	.260
4	.599	.359
5	.659	.434
6	.730	.533
7	.782	.612
8	.839	.704
9	.884	.781
12	1.031	1.063
16	1.192	1.421

2. If L = 10 , T^2 = .875
2a. L/T^2 = 11.43
2b. For T measured in seconds and L in paper clips:
   11.43 (T^2) = L.

3. For a 20 clip chain:
   11.43 (T^2) = 20
   T^2 = 1.75
   T = $\sqrt{1.75}$
   T = 1.323 seconds
      (1.342 by exp.)

4. The period of this giant pendulum is 60 seconds:
   L = 11.43 (60^2)
   L = 11.43 (3600)
   L $\cong$ 41,000 clips

Materials

☐ The data table from the previous activity.
☐ A calculator.

☐ Graph paper.
☐ Thread.
☐ An index card or a straightedge.

☐ Paper clips of uniform size.
☐ A stopwatch.

(TO) experimentally calculate square roots using pendulum variables.

SQUARE ROOTS   O   Pendulums ( )

1. In the previous activity you graphed L *vs* T^2 as a straight line. Show that this equation holds true:

$$\sqrt{\frac{L_1}{L_2}} = \frac{T_1}{T_2}$$

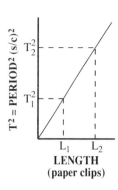

2. Use these ratios to experimentally determine the square root of 2. Then multiply your result by itself. How close did you get to 2?

3. Use your pendulum data to find the square root of 5.

13

Answers / Notes

1. *Pre-algebra students can demonstrate this equality by substituting values for L and T from their graph (or data table) in activity 11. Algebra students might start with the ratio they calculated in step 2a of activity 12.*

<u>pre-algebra</u>

$$\sqrt{\frac{L_1}{L_2}} = \frac{T_1}{T_2}$$

$$\sqrt{\frac{4}{8}} = \frac{.599}{.839}$$

$$\sqrt{.5} = .714$$

$$.707 \cong .714$$

<u>algebra</u>

$$\frac{L_1}{T_1{}^2} = \frac{L_2}{T_2{}^2} = 11.43$$

$$L_1 T_2{}^2 = L_2 T_1{}^2$$

$$\frac{L_1}{L_2} = \frac{T_1{}^2}{T_2{}^2}$$

$$\sqrt{\frac{L_1}{L_2}} = \frac{T_1}{T_2}$$

2. *To calculate $\sqrt{2}$, divide the period of any pendulum by the period of another pendulum that is half its length:*

$$\sqrt{\frac{L_1}{L_2}} = \frac{T_1}{T_2}$$

$$\sqrt{\frac{8}{4}} = \frac{.839}{.599} \genfrac{}{}{0pt}{}{}{} \text{Activity 11 or 12}$$

$$\sqrt{2} = 1.401$$

Check:
  1.401 x 1.401 = 1.96
This result is reasonably close to two.

3.
$$\sqrt{\frac{L_1}{L_2}} = \frac{T_1}{T_2}$$

$$\sqrt{\frac{20}{4}} = \frac{1.342}{.599} \nearrow \text{Activity 12, step 3}$$

$$\sqrt{5} = 2.240$$

Check:
  2.240 x 2.240 = 5.02
This result is reasonably close to five.

Materials

☐ Results from activities 11 or 12.
☐ A calculator.

(TO) study how pendulums receive energy pulses at simple multiplies of their own natural frequency.

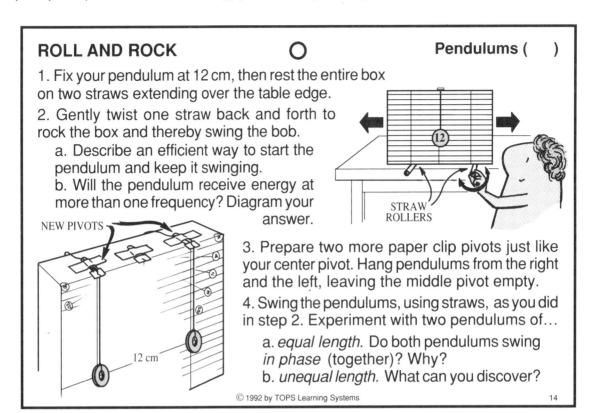

ROLL AND ROCK ○ Pendulums (   )

1. Fix your pendulum at 12 cm, then rest the entire box on two straws extending over the table edge.

2. Gently twist one straw back and forth to rock the box and thereby swing the bob.
   a. Describe an efficient way to start the pendulum and keep it swinging.
   b. Will the pendulum receive energy at more than one frequency? Diagram your answer.

NEW PIVOTS

12 cm

STRAW ROLLERS

3. Prepare two more paper clip pivots just like your center pivot. Hang pendulums from the right and the left, leaving the middle pivot empty.

4. Swing the pendulums, using straws, as you did in step 2. Experiment with two pendulums of…
   a. *equal length*. Do both pendulums swing *in phase* (together)? Why?
   b. *unequal length*. What can you discover?

© 1992 by TOPS Learning Systems   14

Answers / Notes

2a. Rock the straw back and forth in time with the frequency of the pendulum, giving it an energy pulse at the top of each swing.

2b. Yes. The pendulum also efficiently absorbs energy at lower frequencies when a pulse is delivered after every third swing, every fifth swing, etc.

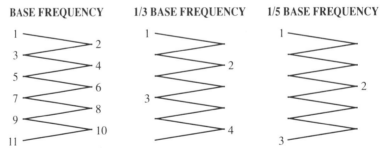

BASE FREQUENCY   1/3 BASE FREQUENCY   1/5 BASE FREQUENCY

4a. Yes. It is relatively easy to keep pendulums of equal length swinging in phase, because both have the same frequency. Simply deliver energy pulses in time with their common frequency.

4b. The pendulum receiving energy pulses timed to its natural frequency steadily increases in amplitude. The other pendulum with a different frequency, is alternately driven, then dampened, as these energy pulses arrive in and out of phase. Thus, as one of the straws swings with higher and higher amplitudes, the other just gets started, then stops, starts and stops, in a repeating cycle.

Materials

☐ The pendulum box with washer pendulum.
☐ Two straws, two washers, two paper clips.
☐ Masking tape.
☐ Scissors.
☐ Thread.

(TO) transfer energy between pendulums of equal and unequal length. To account for observed differences in terms of frequency and phase.

ENERGY BRIDGE ⭕ Pendulums ( )

1. Fix two pendulum bobs at 12 cm. Use a 15 cm piece of straw to bridge the pendulums at the 3 cm level. Cut matching slits in the ends to hold the threads so they hang straight.

    a. Start one bob swinging while the other hangs motionless. What happens?

    b. Do both pendulums move exactly in phase or is one slightly ahead? Look closely.

    c. Will the pendulums transfer energy if you swing them together, exactly in phase? Why?

    d. What happens as you raise or lower the "energy bridge?"

2. Lengthen the left pendulum to 15 cm, leaving the right bob at 12 cm.

    a. Swing one bob while the other remains at rest. What happens now?

    b. Why do pendulums with unequal lengths behave differently?

3. Carefully peel off the right and left paper clip pivots. Leave the center pivot in place.

© 1992 by TOPS Learning Systems

15

Answers / Notes

1a. The pendulums shift their energy of motion back and forth through the straw. As one decays to a stop, the other reaches maximum amplitude. Then the process reverses.

1b. The "pushing" pendulum swings *into* its stationary neighbor, swinging slightly ahead as it transfers energy. Once stopped, it becomes the "receiving" pendulum, lagging somewhat behind as it gets pushed by its neighbor.

1c. No. If both pendulums move exactly in phase, the washers and connecting straw slow together. Neither pendulum pushes nor gets pushed by the other. *(Similarly, no energy is transferred if the pendulums move exactly out of phase.)*

1d. Energy transfers more rapidly between the pendulums as the straw is lowered; more slowly as it is raised. *(Pushing the thread near each bob has more effect than pushing near the pivots.)*

2a. The pendulum you swing first transfers only part of its energy before gaining it back again. It slows down and speeds up while the other (originally at rest) starts and stops.

2b. The pendulum originally set in motion starts pushing against is unequal stationary neighbor. Before it can transfer very much energy, this neighbor, swinging at a different frequency, moves from a delayed "receiving" phase to an advanced "pushing" phase, thus yielding back again the little energy it received.

Materials

☐ The pendulum box from the previous activity with two washer pendulums.
☐ A plastic straw.
☐ Scissors.

(TO) examine a pendulum system with two distinct pivot points. To develop an equation for calculating its period.

TWO-PIVOT PENDULUM ○ Pendulums ( )

1. Center a pendulum at 14 cm on your box. Stick a straight pin firmly into your box at the 6 cm dot, to the *right* of the thread.

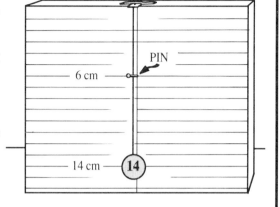

2. Pendulums swing about a fixed point called the pivot. Swing this pendulum and watch it move. Identify its pivot points.

3. Think of a way to calculate the period of this pendulum based on the periods of other pendulums you have already measured. Explain your reasoning.

4. Verify your prediction with a stopwatch.

5. Write an equation to show how these pendulum periods are related:

$$T_{\text{TWO-PIVOT}} \qquad T_{\text{LONGER}} \qquad T_{\text{SHORTER}}$$

Show that your equation holds true for a different combination of pendulums.

© 1992 by TOPS Learning Systems

16

Answers / Notes

2. Over the left half of the pendulum's swing, its pivot is located at the top paper clip, 14 cm from the middle of the bob. Over the right half of its swing the thread wraps around the pin, thus forming a new pivot located 8 cm from the middle of the bob.

3. This two-pivot pendulum has a length of 14 cm through half its swing, then 8 cm through its other half. Its overall period, therefore, may be the average of the periods for these two lengths:

$$\begin{array}{r} T_{8\,\text{CM}} = \quad .574 \text{ s/c} \\ \underline{T_{14\,\text{CM}} = \quad .757 \text{ s/c}} \\ 1.331 \text{ s/c} \end{array} \qquad T_{\text{AVG}} = \frac{1.331 \text{ s/c}}{2} = .666 \text{ s/c}$$

4. When timed with a stopwatch the two-pivot pendulum took 6.60 seconds to complete 10 full cycles, yielding a period of .660 s/c. This value agrees with the calculated value in step 3, well within reasonable limits of experimental error.

5. $$T_{\text{TWO-PIVOT}} = \frac{T_{\text{LONGER}} + T_{\text{SHORTER}}}{2}$$

Students should reinsert the pin at any new position and/or change the length of the washer pendulum, then recalculate its period with the averaging formula and confirm its period with a stopwatch.

Materials

☐ The pendulum box.
☐ A straight pin.
☐ The data table from activity 5 or 9.
☐ A stopwatch.

(TO) study energy transformations in a swinging pendulum. To understand that energy in the bob is always conserved.

CONSERVATION OF ENERGY ○   Pendulums (   )

1. There are 3 tiny bull's-eyes (⊕) on your pendulum box. Stick pins into the two that rest *on* the 7 cm line. Fix the bob at 12 cm.

2. Swing your pendulum from 1 pin stop to the other.
   a. *Potential Energy* is stored in the bob by virtue of its *position*. Where does it have maximum PE?

   b. *Kinetic Energy* is stored in the bob by virtue of its *speed*. Where does it have maximum KE?

   c. As the bob swings, how do these energies change form?

   d. If you release the bob while it touches the left pin, does it usually recover enough potential energy to touch the right? Why?

3. Raise the left pin to the slightly higher bull's-eye. Repeat step 2d.

4. Center a pivot pin inside the 7 cm circle to the right of the thread. Will the edge of the washer still reach the 7 cm line? Use a fourth pin stop to find out.

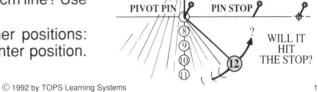

5. Move the pivot pin to other positions: circle 5, circle 10, any off-center position. What always seems true?

© 1992 by TOPS Learning Systems   17

Answers / Notes

2a. The bob stores maximum PE at the top of its swing, when touching either pin stop.

2b. The bob stores maximum KE at the bottom of its swing, where it moves the fastest.

2c. On the downswing, the bob's PE decreases to zero at the bottom of the arc while its KE increases to a maximum. On the upswing, the bob's KE decreases to zero at the top of the arc, while its PE increases to a maximum.

2d. Not usually. A small amount of energy is lost to friction as the bob pushes through air and lightly brushes the side of the box. Hence its PE (energy of position) is not totally recovered.

3. The extra PE added to the bob by raising it slightly higher more than compensates for the energy lost to friction during one swing. Enough KE remains to boost the bob high enough to strike the right pin stop.

4. This 2-pivot pendulum has just enough energy to swing back up to the 7 cm level and strike a pin stop at that height.

5. Neglecting small amounts of energy lost to friction, the bob retains its PE, returning to the same height at all pivot-pin locations. If this pivot pin is positioned too low, however, so the bob is constrained from reaching the 7 cm level by a short "leash", unused KE carries it over the top in a loop-the-loop.

Demonstration

Fill a gallon milk jug with water and cap it. Tie nylon fishing line or heavy string to its handle, then hang this pendulum from a sturdy ceiling fixture. Adjust for length so the water jug approaches your face as you stand with your back against the wall. Turn the jug so its leading edge *almost* touches your face, then release it (without shoving!). The conservation of energy is your insurance policy that the water jug can't smack you in the face on its return trip.

Materials

☐ The pendulum box.
☐ Straight pins.

(TO) graphically analyze how energy in a pendulum system changes forms.

ENERGY CURVE ◯ Pendulums (   )

1. Hang the washer to rest at 12 cm on your pendulum box.

    a. What is its PE? (Notice that this energy, defined in *joule* units or "J", is written to the left on the box.)

    b. Now center your pendulum on the next higher energy level (.0005 J). What is its amplitude for this PE?

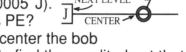

    c. Complete this data table: center the bob at each higher energy level to find the amplitude at that level. (The washer's hole centers on *lines*, not circles.)

2. Plot your data on a full sheet of graph paper numbered as shown. Label your energy curve "PE".

3. Swing your pendulum at 60° maximum amplitude. Roll straws to add energy, as in activity 14.

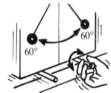

    a. Apply your graph to this 60° pendulum. What can you say about its changing PE?

    b. Draw a KE curve for this 60° pendulum on the same graph. Explain your reasoning.

AMPLI-TUDE (°)	ENERGY (joules)
0	.0000
24	.0005
	.0010
	.0015
⋮	⋮
90	.0060

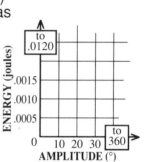

© 1992 by TOPS Learning Systems

18

Answers / Notes

1. *If your students have studied about energy and work, ask them to verify that the energy units on this scale have the correct order of magnitude: washers that fit quarter inch bolts typically have a mass of about 5 grams, weighing about .05 newtons. To raise the washer from 12 cm to 11 cm thus requires a force of .05 N applied though a distance of .01 meters. The work done, or gain in potential energy, is .05 N x .01 m = .0005 joule for each energy level.*

1a. Hanging motionless, the pendulum has no potential energy (0 J or 0 joules).

1b. 24°

1c.

AMPLITUDE (°)	ENERGY (joules)
0	.0000
24	.0005
33	.0010
41	.0015
48	.0020
54	.0025
60	.0030
65	.0035
70	.0040
76	.0045
80	.0050
85	.0055
90	.0060

Materials

☐ The pendulum box.
☐ Graph paper.
☐ Two straws.

2. *For now, the graph occupies only the lower left quarter of the graph paper. It will be extended in the next activity.*

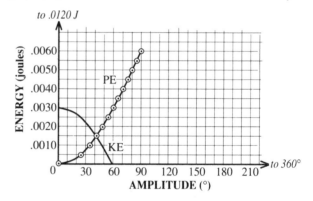

3a. On the upswing, the bob stores PE first slowly, then more rapidly as the amplitude increases. It stops at 60° with .0030 J of energy. On the downswing, the bob releases its PE first rapidly, then more slowly as the amplitude decreases, At the bottom of the swing, the bob has lost all PE.

3b. Total energy in the system (PE + KE) remains constant, since the pendulum swings at a steady 60° maximum amplitude with small infusions of energy from the straw. The KE curve, therefore, is plotted so the sum of both energy forms always equals .0030 J. *(One curve is the mirror image of the other.)*

(TO) graph the energy of a washer that revolves full circle. To compare this system to a low-amplitude pendulum.

IN ORBIT Pendulums ( )

1. Imagine standing a second pendulum box upside down on the first, to form a full 360° circle. Continue graphing amplitude *vs* PE for a 12 cm pendulum all the way around.

2. Release the washer at the top of your energy curve. How well does your pendulum system retain its full .0120 J of energy? Describe the energy conversions you observe.

3. What parts of your bell curve apply to smoothly swinging pendulums? Explain.

4. Make a 12 cm "loop" pendulum as measured from the center of the washer to the center of the straw. (The finished loop is about 25 cm around. Measure extra length to tie a knot.)

5. Use both hands to *slowly* twirl the bob in a smooth circle, just fast enough to carry it over the top without jerking the thread.

    a. Does PE in this revolving washer match your bell curve? Explain.

    b. Does KE equal 0 at the top of the arc? Explain.

    c. Would you expect this washer to have the same period when it "orbits" as when it swings? Explain.

    d. Test your hypothesis.

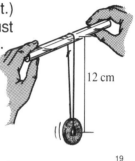

19

Answers / Notes

1. *An easy way to complete this graph is to plot easily determined energy levels at a few key amplitudes — 120°, 180°, 240°, 270°, 300° — then fill in the lines between these points guided by symmetry. The resulting "bell" curve is defined by a multiple of 1– cos ø.*

2. Released at 180° with maximum PE, the washer free-falls through a distance of 24 cm, perhaps striking the the box on the way down. Its .0120 J of energy shakes the whole box and produces sound. Only a tiny fraction of this energy is retained by the pendulum, swinging it just a few degrees of amplitude beyond 0 joules.

3. Only the lower parts of the bell-shaped curve, below 90° amplitude (or above 270°), apply to smooth pendulum motion. When the washer stops at positions higher than this, it free-falls from loose thread, instead of retracing its normal pendulum arc.

5a. Yes. The bell curve tracks changes in the washer's PE over 1 full revolution. Its PE increases from zero, up one side of the curve to a maximum on top, then curves back to zero on the other side.

5b. No. If the washer had no KE at the top of its arc it would stop and fall straight down.

5c. No. This orbiting washer requires additional

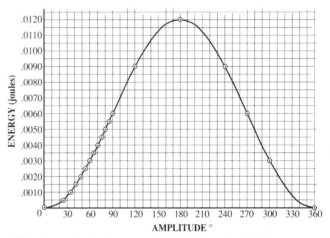

KE to keep it circling smoothly. This extra KE increases the washer's velocity, which shortens its period.

5d. The minimum period required to keep the washer circling smoothly is about .458 s/c. This is significantly less than .702 s/c, its period when swinging at low amplitudes as a normal pendulum.

Materials

☐ The pendulum box.   ☐ A centimeter ruler. Photocopy
☐ Thread and washer.   this from the supplementary
☐ Scissors.   page. Or use a meter stick.
☐ A straw.   ☐ A stopwatch.

(TO) calculate the refresh rate of a video screen in hertz units.

IT'S REFRESHING

Pendulums ( )

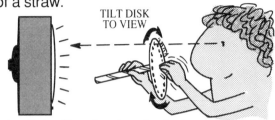

1. Poke a pin exactly through the center bump of a plastic lid, *up* from below. Poke another pin 4 mm off center, down from above. Watch out for fingers!

2. Cut out the paper disk (with small flag), then accurately punch out all black holes around its edge. Poke the top (centered) pin exactly through the disk's center.

3. Fasten paper disk to plastic lid with 2 pieces of tape rolled sticky-side out.

4. Drop the centered pin into the end of a straw.
   a. Practice twirling the off-center pin to rapidly spin the disk, then let it coast to a stop.
   b. Do this while looking through its holes at a working video screen. Make careful observations.

5. The screen flashes rapidly, like a strobe light, illuminating the holes in a series of separate "snapshots." Explain how this "stops" the holes on your spinning disk.

6. Calculate the frequency of the screen's *refresh rate* in hertz . Work with a friend.

20

Answers / Notes

1. *The safest way do this is to poke both holes* before *fully inserting the pins.*

4b. As the rapidly spinning disk gradually slows, its normal spacing of holes (1x) appears to move forward, then stop, then move backward in what resembles a "rocking" cycle. The hole pattern then "flips" into what appears to be a rocking cycle for quadruple the holes (4x), twice the holes (2x), then 4x, 1x, 4x, 2x, 4x, stop.

5. The screen briefly illuminates the punched holes in the disk during each flash, but not between flashes. At just the right rotational speeds, successive snapshots superimpose to freeze the action at different multiples of holes. To "freeze" a *normal* spacing of holes at the slowest speed, for example, each hole turns just far enough between flashes to appear exactly where its neighbor appeared in the previous snapshot. Holes can superimpose at multiples of this basic speed, as well.

6. *One student should spin the disk at a steady rate, just fast enough to "freeze" the normal spacing of holes at the slowest disk speed. A lab partner should then time the period of rotation with a stopwatch, counting 10 revolutions of the "flag" attached to the disk. Here is a result for our computer screen:*

   10 revolutions of disk = 5.98 seconds
   1 period of disk= .598 seconds
   There are 45 holes in the disk. The time required for the disk to rotate from one hole to the next is .598 seconds/45, or .0133 seconds. The screen flashes over this same time interval to freeze the holes. Thus,
   refresh period = .0133 s/c
   refresh frequency = 1/refresh period = 75.25 Hz.
   (actual refresh frequency = 75 Hz)

Extension

Can you get similar results by turning the disk at other frequencies? By using a variable speed mixer or hand-operated egg beater?

Materials

☐ A plastic lid with a bump that defines its center. Find this on coffee, margarine or roasted nut products.
☐ Straight pins and masking tape.
☐ A metric ruler.
☐ The paper disk with holes. Photocopy this from the supplementary page.
☐ Scissors and a paper punch.
☐ A plastic straw. Half a straw is sufficient.
☐ A video screen on a television or computer. Refresh rates will vary. An owner's manual should list the frequency of your particular unit.
☐ A stopwatch and a calculator.

---

enrichment

REPRODUCIBLE
STUDENT
TASK CARDS

Task Cards Options

Here are 3 management options to consider before you photocopy:

1. Consumable Worksheets: Copy 1 complete set of task card pages. Cut out each card and fix it to a separate sheet of boldly lined paper. Duplicate a class set of each worksheet master you have made, 1 per student. Direct students to follow the task card instructions at the top of each page, then respond to questions in the lined space underneath.

2. Nonconsumable Reference Booklets: Copy and collate the 2-up task card pages in sequence. Make perhaps half as many sets as the students who will use them. Staple each set in the upper left corner, both front and back to prevent the outside pages from working loose. Tell students that these task card booklets are for reference only. They should use them as they would any textbook, responding to questions on their own papers, returning them unmarked and in good shape at the end of the module.

3. Nonconsumable Task Cards: Copy several sets of task card pages. Laminate them, if you wish, for extra durability, then cut out each card to display in your room. You might pin cards to bulletin boards; or punch out the holes and hang them from wall hooks (you can fashion hooks from paper clips and tape these to the wall); or fix cards to cereal boxes with paper fasteners, 4 to a box; or keep cards on designated reference tables. The important thing is to provide enough task card reference points about your classroom to avoid a jam of too many students at any one location. Two or 3 task card sets should accommodate everyone, since different students will use different cards at different times.

PENDULUM BOX O   Pendulums (   )

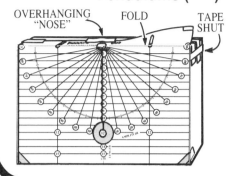

1. Fill an empty cereal box about 1/6 full of gravel. Tape it closed, then tip it on its side.

2. Cut out the Pendulum Grid. Fold it back on the dotted line to fit neatly over the upper edge of your box. Tape in place.

3. Fold a tab of tape over the double-loop end of a paper clip. *Lightly* tape it to the center top of the box with its taped "nose" sticking out.

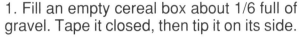

4. Tie thread to a washer. Insert this thread into a slit that you cut in the tape tab to the center "nose" of the clip. Tilt the box forward to let the washer unwind.

5. Tape the thread at the top of the box so its washer centers perfectly over the 12 cm circle (adjust the clip as needed). Now release your pendulum at an *amplitude* of 10°.

    a. Check that the pendulum swings for at least 1 minute without stopping. Adjust, if necessary, for minimum friction with maximum closeness to the box. Then tape the clip (not the pendulum thread) firmly in place.

    b. Write your name on top.

    1

FREQUENCY O   Pendulums (   )

1. Set the center of the washer over the 15 cm circle. Secure the thread at the top with tape. Start the pendulum swinging with an amplitude of 20°.

    a. Find its *frequency*, the number of *cycles* the pendulum makes in 1 minute.

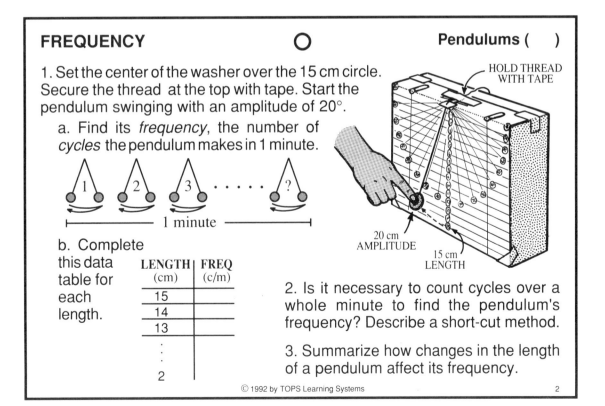

b. Complete this data table for each length.

LENGTH (cm)	FREQ (c/m)
15	
14	
13	
:	
:	
:	
2	

2. Is it necessary to count cycles over a whole minute to find the pendulum's frequency? Describe a short-cut method.

3. Summarize how changes in the length of a pendulum affect its frequency.

    2

LENGTH *vs* FREQUENCY   Pendulums (   )

1 Hz = 1 c/s

1. Frequency is usually measured in units called *hertz* (Hz). If a pendulum vibrates 1 cycle every second, it has a frequency of 1 Hz.

    a. A pendulum has a frequency of 1.5 Hz. How many cycles does it complete in 1 minute?

    b. A pendulum has a frequency of 77 c/m. What is its frequency in hertz units?

2. Copy your results from the last activity into a new table. Then convert the frequency for each pendulum length from cycles/minute to hertz units.

LENGTH (cm)	FREQ (c/m)	FREQ (Hz=c/s)
15		
14		
13		
.		
.		
2		

3. Graph length (in cm) *vs* frequency (in Hz).

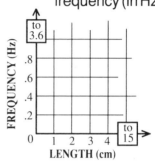

3

PERIOD   Pendulums (   )

1. Fix the length of your pendulum at 15 cm.

    a. Use a stopwatch to time the number of seconds required to complete 10 cycles. Practice until you consistently get the same result within a range of .10 second.

    b. Complete the middle column of the data table for each length.

HOLD AMPLITUDE TO 20° OR LESS.

LENGTH (cm)	TIME for 10 cycles (s)	PERIOD (s/c)
15		
14		
13		
.		
.		
2		

2. The *period* of a pendulum is the time (in seconds) needed to complete 1 cycle. Enter the period for each length in column 3.

$$\text{Period} = \frac{\text{no. of seconds}}{\text{1 cycle}}$$

3. Summarize how changes in the length of a pendulum affects its period. Is this how length affects frequency?

4

LENGTH *vs* PERIOD　　　　○　　　　Pendulums (　)

1. Copy your results from the last two activities into a new data table with *increasing* lengths.

2. How are frequencies and periods related? Experiment by dividing each of them into 1. What do you notice?

3. Write an equation that relates frequency to period; period to frequency.

4. Make a graph as shown, with extra length for later use. Plot *length vs period*, then draw a smooth curve.

5. Compare this graph line to its *inverse* in activity 3. What do you see?

6. Remember how you measured the data in columns 2 and 3. Which measurements do you think contain less experimental error? Explain.

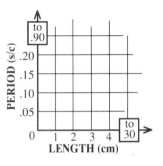

LENGTH (cm)	FREQ. (c/s=Hz)	PERIOD (s/c)
0	—	0
2		
3		
⋮		
15		

Activity 3, last column → FREQ.
Activity 4, last column → PERIOD

5

AMPLITUDE & BOB WEIGHT　　　　○　　　　Pendulums (　)

1. Set your pendulum at 12 cm.
   a. Measure the period of this pendulum when released at each angle of amplitude. Time 10 cycles with a stopwatch as before, then divide by 10 to compute the period.

AMPLI- TUDE (°)	PERIOD (s/c)
10	
30	
50	
70	
90	

   b. Do changing *amplitudes* affect a pendulum's period? How does this compare to changing *length*?

MASS OF BOB　　AMPLITUDE　　LENGTH

2. Reset your pendulum at 16 cm.
   a. Add extra washers to the pendulum bob with small rolls of tape. Time the periods for different bob weights when released at a constant 20° amplitude.

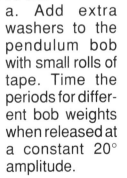
ROLLED TAPE

BOB WEIGHT (washers)	PERIOD (s/c)
1	
2	
3	
4	
5	

   b. Do changes in *bob weight* affect a pendulum's period? Explain.

3. Summarize how these three *variables* affect the period of a pendulum.

6

BOINGGG! ○   Pendulums (   )

1. Wrap 1 meter of thin wire evenly around a size-D battery to make a coil spring.

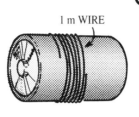

1 m WIRE

2. Pull out the arm of a paper clip a little to form a hook. Attach it to one end of your spring.

3. Clamp the other end of your spring to a clothespin that is taped on your cereal box. Set the box at the edge of your table so the spring falls over the edge.

4. Investigate how different variables (bob weight, length, etc.) affect the period of a spring pendulum. Compare your result to washer pendulums. Your write-up should include at least 1 graph.

VARIABLES?

5. Carefully remove the clothespin from your pendulum box when you finish.

7

EXTRAPOLATE ○   Pendulums (   )

1. Extrapolate (extend) your graph line in activity 5 with a dashed line: draw your best guess based on how the curve seems to change.

2. Based on your extrapolation, *predict* what pendulum length will tick like a clock — exactly 1 second per cycle.

1 s/c

PERIOD (s/c)

EXTRAPOLATE

LENGTH (cm)   ?

3. Fold a tape handle *loosely* over thread tied to a washer. Slide it to make a "clock" pendulum with your predicted length, as measured from the center of the bob to the edge of the tape (called the *pivot*).

TAPE HANDLE ← *SLIDE ALONG THREAD* →

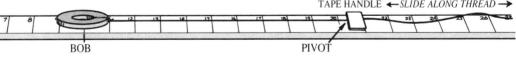

BOB   PIVOT

a. Swing this pendulum clock by its tape pivot. How close does it come to ticking 1 s/c?

b. Slide the pivot up or down until your "clock" keeps good time. Record its length as a hard data point on your graph.

4. Change your pendulum's length to locate 2 more hard data points in the extrapolated area of your graph. Evaluate the accuracy of your extrapolation. (*Don't* redraw your dashed line.)

8

SQUARE IT   ○   Pendulums (   )

1. Copy the period data from activity 5 into this new table:

2. Find the square of each period: use a calculator to multiply the period by itself, then enter each result (to three figures) in column 3.

3. Graph your data from columns 1 and 3.

    a. Your points will distribute into a fairly straight line, with some scattering due to experimental error. Which points do you trust the most? The least? Explain.

    b. Use a thread to draw the best possible straight line among your data points.

4. Each point on your graph line relates a unique pendulum length (L) to the square of its particular period (T^2).

    a. Compute the ratio **L/T²** for T^2 = .20, .40, and .60.

    b. What always seems true?

Activity 5 last column

LENGTH L=cm	PERIOD T=s/c	PERIOD² T²=(s/c)²
0		
2		
3		
⋮		
15		

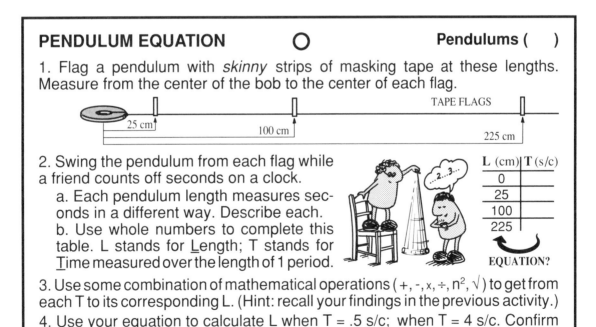

9

PENDULUM EQUATION   ○   Pendulums (   )

1. Flag a pendulum with *skinny* strips of masking tape at these lengths. Measure from the center of the bob to the center of each flag.

TAPE FLAGS

25 cm   100 cm   225 cm

2. Swing the pendulum from each flag while a friend counts off seconds on a clock.

    a. Each pendulum length measures seconds in a different way. Describe each.

    b. Use whole numbers to complete this table. L stands for <u>L</u>ength; T stands for <u>T</u>ime measured over the length of 1 period.

...2...3...

L (cm)	T (s/c)
0	
25	
100	
225	

EQUATION?

3. Use some combination of mathematical operations ($+, -, \times, \div, n^2, \sqrt{}$) to get from each T to its corresponding L. (Hint: recall your findings in the previous activity.)

4. Use your equation to calculate L when T = .5 s/c; when T = 4 s/c. Confirm at least one of your results by experiment; both, if possible.

5. Imagine launching off on a 1 km rope swing hanging from a sky hook. How many seconds would you ride before returning to your starting point?

10

CHAIN LINKS (1)   O   Pendulums ( )

1. Paper clips link to make a chain pendulum. Develop a data table and graph to explore the relationship between length (in paper clips) and period (in s/c).

THIS IS A
6 CLIP
CHAIN:

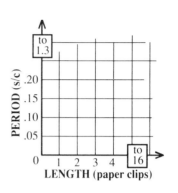

2. How do your results compare with the washer pendulum you studied earlier?

11

CHAIN LINKS (2)   O   Pendulums ( )

1. Determine how the length (L) of a paper-clip chain varies directly with the square of its period (T^2). Develop a data table and graph.

2. If L = 10 clips, read T^2 from your graph.
a. Find the ratio L/T^2 on a calculator.
b. Recall the equation you developed for a washer pendulum. Write a similar equation for paper-clip pendulums.

3. Use your equation to find the frequency of a 20 clip chain. Verify your answer with a stopwatch.

4. How many paper clips should you link together to make a chain that requires 1 whole minute to complete just 1 cycle?

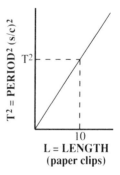

12

SQUARE ROOTS　　　　О　　　　Pendulums (　　)

1. In the previous activity you graphed L *vs* T^2 as a straight line. Show that this equation holds true:

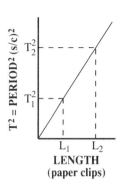

$$\sqrt{\frac{L_1}{L_2}} = \frac{T_1}{T_2}$$

2. Use these ratios to experimentally determine the square root of 2. Then multiply your result by itself. How close did you get to 2?

3. Use your pendulum data to find the square root of 5.

13

ROLL AND ROCK　　　　О　　　　Pendulums (　　)

1. Fix your pendulum at 12 cm, then rest the entire box on two straws extending over the table edge.

2. Gently twist one straw back and forth to rock the box and thereby swing the bob.

   a. Describe an efficient way to start the pendulum and keep it swinging.

   b. Will the pendulum receive energy at more than one frequency? Diagram your answer.

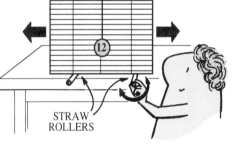

STRAW ROLLERS

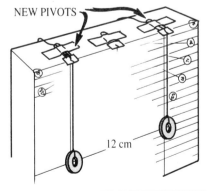

NEW PIVOTS

12 cm

3. Prepare two more paper clip pivots just like your center pivot. Hang pendulums from the right and the left, leaving the middle pivot empty.

4. Swing the pendulums, using straws, as you did in step 2. Experiment with two pendulums of…

   a. *equal length.* Do both pendulums swing *in phase* (together)? Why?

   b. *unequal length.* What can you discover?

14

ENERGY BRIDGE Pendulums (   )

1. Fix two pendulum bobs at 12 cm. Use a 15 cm piece of straw to bridge the pendulums at the 3 cm level. Cut matching slits in the ends to hold the threads so they hang straight.

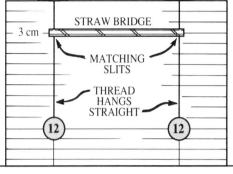

   a. Start one bob swinging while the other hangs motionless. What happens?
   b. Do both pendulums move exactly in phase or is one slightly ahead? Look closely.
   c. Will the pendulums transfer energy if you swing them together, exactly in phase? Why?
   d. What happens as you raise or lower the "energy bridge?"

2. Lengthen the left pendulum to 15 cm, leaving the right bob at 12 cm.

   a. Swing one bob while the other remains at rest. What happens now?
   b. Why do pendulums with unequal lengths behave differently?

3. Carefully peel off the right and left paper clip pivots. Leave the center pivot in place.

© 1992 by TOPS Learning Systems

15

TWO-PIVOT PENDULUM Pendulums (   )

1. Center a pendulum at 14 cm on your box. Stick a straight pin firmly into your box at the 6 cm dot, to the *right* of the thread.

2. Pendulums swing about a fixed point called the pivot. Swing this pendulum and watch it move. Identify its pivot points.

3. Think of a way to calculate the period of this pendulum based on the periods of other pendulums you have already measured. Explain your reasoning.

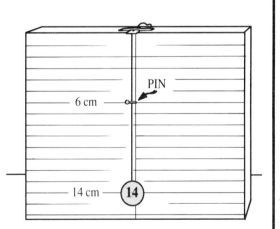

4. Verify your prediction with a stopwatch.

5. Write an equation to show how these pendulum periods are related:

$$T_{\text{TWO-PIVOT}} \qquad T_{\text{LONGER}} \qquad T_{\text{SHORTER}}$$

Show that your equation holds true for a different combination of pendulums.

© 1992 by TOPS Learning Systems

16

CONSERVATION OF ENERGY ⭘   Pendulums ( )

1. There are 3 tiny bull's-eyes (⊕) on your pendulum box. Stick pins into the two that rest *on* the 7 cm line. Fix the bob at 12 cm.

2. Swing your pendulum from 1 pin stop to the other.

a. *Potential Energy* is stored in the bob by virtue of its *position*. Where does it have maximum PE?

b. *Kinetic Energy* is stored in the bob by virtue of its *speed*. Where does it have maximum KE?

c. As the bob swings, how do these energies change form?

d. If you release the bob while it touches the left pin, does it usually recover enough potential energy to touch the right? Why?

3. Raise the left pin to the slightly higher bull's-eye. Repeat step 2d.

4. Center a pivot pin inside the 7 cm circle to the right of the thread. Will the edge of the washer still reach the 7 cm line? Use a fourth pin stop to find out.

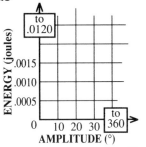

PIVOT PIN   PIN STOP

WILL IT HIT THE STOP?

5. Move the pivot pin to other positions: circle 5, circle 10, any off-center position. What always seems true?

    17

ENERGY CURVE ⭘   Pendulums ( )

1. Hang the washer to rest at 12 cm on your pendulum box.

AMPLI- TUDE (°)	ENERGY (joules)
0	.0000
24	.0005
	.0010
	.0015
⋮	⋮
90	.0060

a. What is its PE? (Notice that this energy, defined in *joule* units or "J", is written to the left on the box.)

b. Now center your pendulum on the next higher energy level (.0005 J). What is its amplitude for this PE?

NEXT LEVEL   CENTER

c. Complete this data table: center the bob at each higher energy level to find the amplitude at that level. (The washer's hole centers on *lines*, not circles.)

2. Plot your data on a full sheet of graph paper numbered as shown. Label your energy curve "PE".

3. Swing your pendulum at 60° maximum amplitude. Roll straws to add energy, as in activity 14.

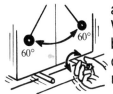

a. Apply your graph to this 60° pendulum. What can you say about its changing PE?

b. Draw a KE curve for this 60° pendulum on the same graph. Explain your reasoning.

ENERGY (joules): to .0120, .0015, .0010, .0005, 0

AMPLITUDE (°): 0 10 20 30 to 360

    18

IN ORBIT   O   Pendulums (   )

1. Imagine standing a second pendulum box upside down on the first, to form a full 360° circle. Continue graphing amplitude *vs* PE for a 12 cm pendulum all the way around.

2. Release the washer at the top of your energy curve. How well does your pendulum system retain its full .0120 J of energy? Describe the energy conversions you observe.

3. What parts of your bell curve apply to smoothly swinging pendulums? Explain.

4. Make a 12 cm "loop" pendulum as measured from the center of the washer to the center of the straw. (The finished loop is about 25 cm around. Measure extra length to tie a knot.)

5. Use both hands to *slowly* twirl the bob in a smooth circle, just fast enough to carry it over the top without jerking the thread.

    a. Does PE in this revolving washer match your bell curve? Explain.

    b. Does KE equal 0 at the top of the arc? Explain.

    c. Would you expect this washer to have the same period when it "orbits" as when it swings? Explain.

    d. Test your hypothesis.

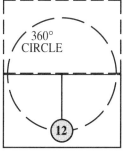

19

IT'S REFRESHING   O   Pendulums (   )

1. Poke a pin exactly through the center bump of a plastic lid, *up* from below. Poke another pin 4 mm off center, down from above. Watch out for fingers!

2. Cut out the paper disk (with small flag), then accurately punch out all black holes around its edge. Poke the top (centered) pin exactly through the disk's center.

3. Fasten paper disk to plastic lid with 2 pieces of tape rolled sticky-side out.

4. Drop the centered pin into the end of a straw.

    a. Practice twirling the off-center pin to rapidly spin the disk, then let it coast to a stop.

    b. Do this while looking through its holes at a working video screen. Make careful observations.

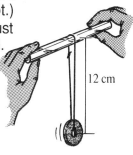

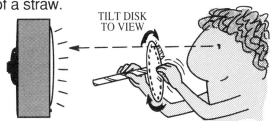

5. The screen flashes rapidly, like a strobe light, illuminating the holes in a series of separate "snapshots." Explain how this "stops" the holes on your spinning disk.

6. Calculate the frequency of the screen's *refresh rate* in hertz . Work with a friend.

20

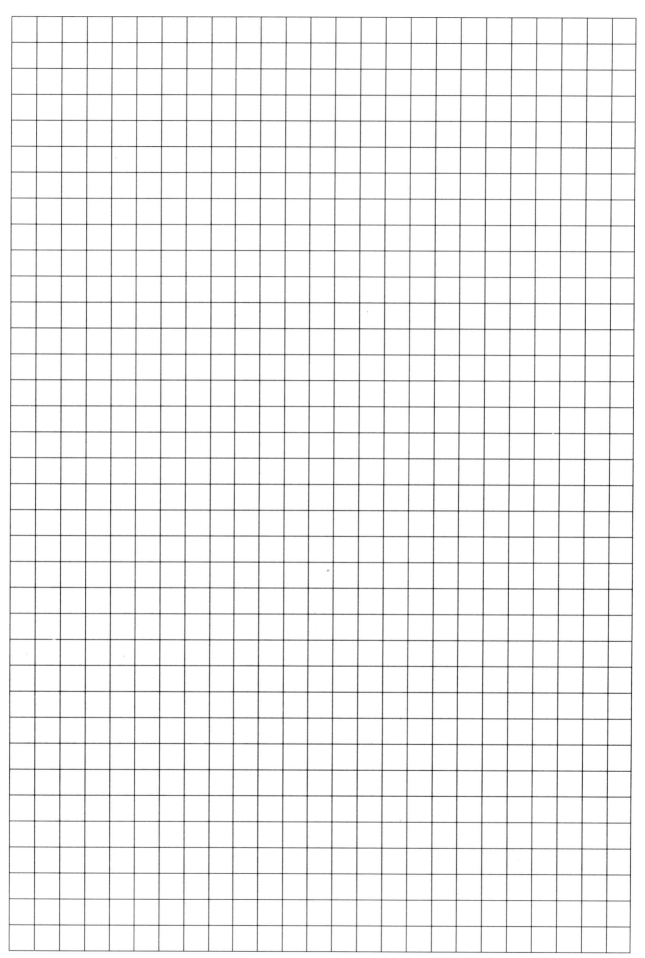

Copyright © 1992 by TOPS Learning Systems.

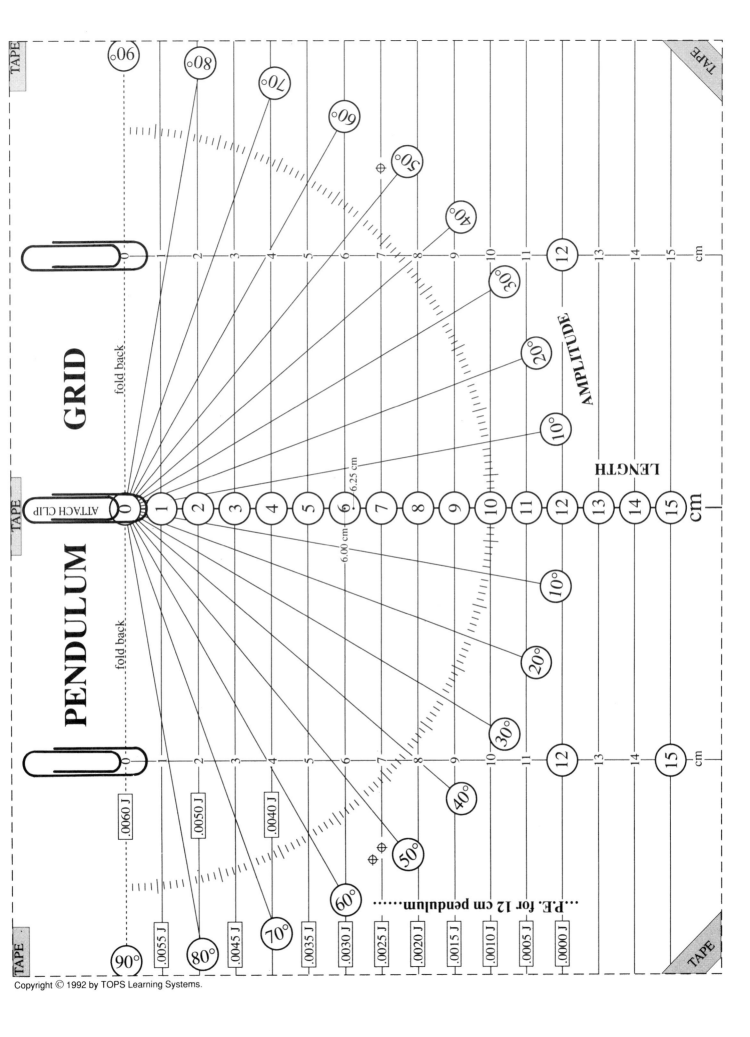

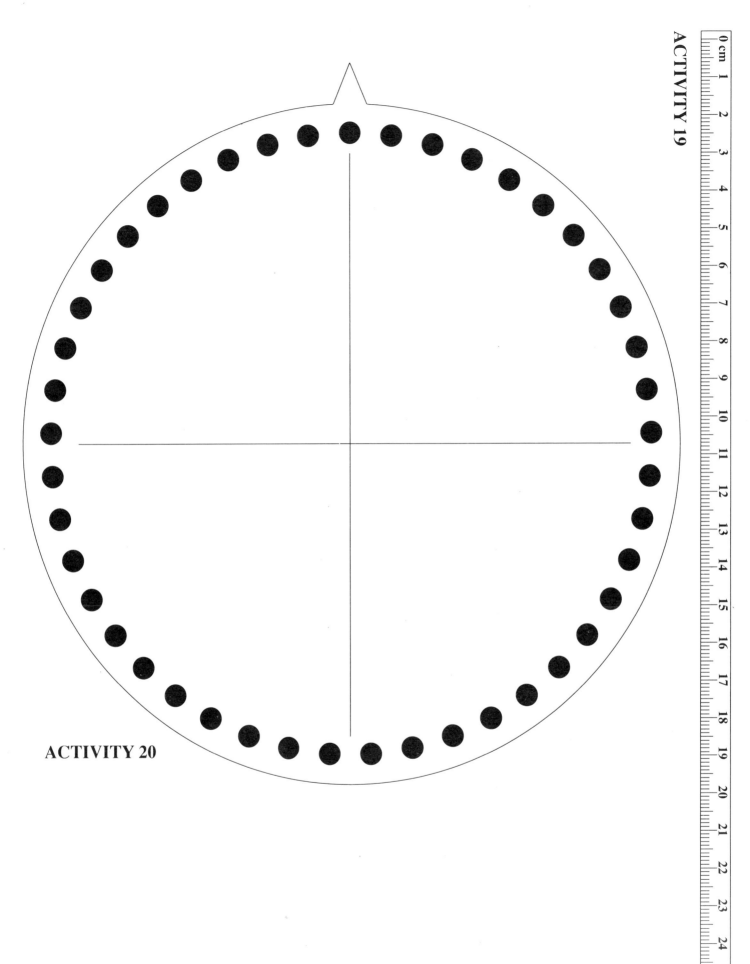

ACTIVITY 20